READY, SET,
Count

Also in the Ready, Set, Learn series:

Ready, Set, Read and Write

Ready, Set, Explore

Ready, Set, Cooperate

READY, SET,
Count

Marlene Barron

with
Karen Romano Young

A Skylight Press Book

John Wiley & Sons, Inc.
New York • Chichester • Brisbane • Toronto • Singapore

To my grandchildren, Sarah, Alexander, and Benjamin
—M.B.

To Sam
—K.R.Y.

Published by John Wiley & Sons, Inc.

All rights reserved. Published simultaneously in Canada.
Published by arrangement with Skylight Press, 260 West 72nd St., Suite 6C,
New York, NY 10023

The publisher and the author have made every reasonable effort
to ensure that the experiments and activities in the book are safe when
conducted as instructed but assume no responsibility for any damage
caused or sustained while performing the experiments or activities in this
book. Parents, guardians, and/or teachers should supervise young readers
who undertake the experiments and activities in this book.

Library of Congress Cataloging-in-Publication Data

Barron, Marlene
    Ready, set, count / Marlene Barron with Karen Romano Young.
        p. cm. — (ready, set, learn series)
    "A Skylight Press book."
    Includes index
    ISBN 0-471-10282-2 (alk. paper)
    1. Mathematics—Study and teaching (Early childhood) 2. Early
childhood education—parent participation. 3. Early childhood
education—Activity programs. I. Young, Karen Romano. II. Title.
III. Series.
QA135.5.B286   1995
649'.68—dc20   95-1306

Printed in the United States of America

10 9 8 7 6 5 4 3 2

Contents

· ·

Introduction

Ages three through seven: these are the years when your child moves from babyhood to childhood and from your lap to formal schooling. During these years, too, your child looks at puppies in a box, cars in a parking lot, and faces in a group, and begins to understand them as numbers—and to express them in numerals as a way to tell "how many." These are vital years for gaining mathematical experiences. Many parents, still shuddering from their own school math, want to give their child a better start. Others who loved math are eager to get their child's feet wet. Your child needs math as part of daily life, play, errands, and family time. You need ideas to foster a love of and a facility with math. Where do you begin? What do you do?

Start here. If you want to help your child see numbers, shapes, patterns, and relationships as tools for building, figuring, solving problems, and creating, you've come to the right place. In this book, you'll find ways to use the daily business of family life—whatever you're doing—to give your child the best possible base for absorbing the mathematical patterns and relationships around him.* You'll find activities that work in tandem with your school's approach, ensuring steady growth and building concepts through experiences.

What's the best way to do math with your child? The creators of many math materials on the market today would have parents believe that their children are empty vessels, waiting to be filled up with data and skills they "need" to move forward in a linear fashion. This attitude is particularly prevalent when it comes to math. But is what they're teaching really math?

In fact, what some people call mathematics is actually arithmetic, a small part of the world of math. Arithmetic is adding, subtracting, multiplying, and dividing numbers. Math is something more. It's the study of the relationships between objects in this world: the intersection of brick and mortar on a wall, the pattern of stripe and shadow created by a picket fence, the structure of the twill of a pair of jeans, the number of fingers on each hand.

* I'll use *he* and *she, his* and *her* interchangeably until the English language evolves a word that means both.

1

No matter what your child's age or stage, she already knows a great many things about math and is ready to build on that knowledge to become as expert at observing and analyzing situations as she is at looking, listening, and asking questions. Children are predisposed, by their inquisitive natures and turned-on powers of observation, to note, organize, and interpret the things they see around them each day. As the director of a Montessori school in New York City, and a longtime specialist in early childhood education, I've seen children come to math understanding in a number of ways. The ones who experience the most success, who carry a love of and a fascination for the shapes, relationships, and patterns of the world, who trust their ability to solve problems, are those whose early years were spent building confidence, exploring, and growing in their understanding of concepts.

This book will show you ways to use math to work and play with your child—any day, in any situation. I have developed these fun, challenging activities during a quarter of a century of teaching and observing the growth of young children, so I know that they work—and that you and your child will enjoy doing them.

While the book contains instructions for each activity, it is open-ended. This means that you can make them your own: use them as starting points, change them as you go along, and end up with a different outcome each time. Through these activities you can create the kind of environment that gives your child plenty of opportunities to learn. Unlike many of the other books designed to prepare children for school, this one does not have lists of required skills, facts, or field trips without which your child will not "measure up." Rather, I'll show you games to use with your three-year-old that will still be a hit when he's six. I'll show you ways to use traffic lights, rocks, playing cards, the hardware store, the TV, doll house furniture, and even the bath water to guide your child into new exploration of math. And I'll show you ways to approach your child's abilities *today* so that you see how he's already solving math problems on his own level.

Each activity is designed to help you give your child experience in one specific area of math. Everything you need is here: a list of materials, a how-to, and an explanation of the activity's purpose. Built into each activity is advice for developing the activity further as your child moves along, for extending it into other areas, and/or for using it with more than one child.

I'm willing to bet that many of these activities will help you become more involved with your child and more confident in your child's natural abilities and talents. You might not use every activity. Try everything, making changes to suit your needs and your child's needs. Make the activities your own, and don't be surprised if you find your enthusiasm for math growing. The goal is to make doing math a beloved, easy, comfortable, and exciting process for you and your child to share together.

Educational Philosophy: Why These Activities Work

Here are some of the general ideas that you'll find throughout the activities.

Whole Math

My preferred approach to the process of learning math is called *whole math*. It incorporates all the ways we use patterns and relationships to make meaning of the world. Meaning-making happens every time a pattern is observed or a relationship noted, at whatever level and in whatever form it occurs: climbing stairs, pushing elevator buttons, turning up the ribbed cuff of a sweater, reading house numbers, walking four blocks, pouring a glass of milk, stroking a cat, picking apples, and making applesauce.

Here's an example of what I mean. How do you teach a child to climb a flight of stairs? You don't! First, she decides on her own that she wants to go up. She figures out that she needs to lift her foot to a certain height, shift her weight to the foot, and lift herself up onto the step. Then she repeats the action over and over until she reaches the top. If you were going to program a robot to walk up a flight of stairs, here's what you'd basically have to do: you'd have to program the robot to determine the number and height of the steps, then to climb that number of steps as it balances its weight accordingly. The robot uses calculations—arithmetic. If it moves from the first flight of stairs to the next one, it has to draw on different calculations. The child, unlike the robot, learns through the whole experience.

She observes, she attempts, she moves and adapts, and she transfers her discovery to other staircases.

It's best for young children to have concrete, physical, sensorial experiences before moving to drawing things out or writing them down. Whole learning takes place everywhere—in the kitchen, bathroom, car, mall, or subway. It is not about teaching skills or trying to instill skills or concepts one by one. It's an all-day, whole-family experience that can't be stuffed into a workbook or an hour of time.

So, how do you get your child involved in making observations, noting patterns, and expressing findings on paper? He already is. A baby begins observing as soon as he focuses his eyes. A child begins to file away specifics, later using them to make generalizations. He notes, for example, that you can't buy too much with pennies; quarters and dollars buy more. He grows to understand that people around him use numbers to get along in the world: assessing distances, pricing food, dialing the telephone, matching mittens, purchasing shoes, telling the time, keeping score, playing cards, building a house, cooking dinner. Surrounded by many uses of numbers, it's natural that he'll develop his own understanding of math concepts.

Just as a child's early, tremulous stair climbing is a precursor to running up the stairs, taking them two at a time, a child's wide-eyed observations are progress toward math proficiency, and her endless questions are a quest to analyze patterns, figure out relationships, and make generalizations. This book offers you the information you need to see your child's progress and to support your child as she moves from looking to purposeful observation, from playing to analyzing, from asking questions to finding answers about mathematical relationships.

Note that many of the activities in this book overlap with other subject areas. Clearly a child who talks his way through a math problem—really a math *situation*—is learning the language required to read and write word problems. A child who generalizes that sidewalks are wider in the city center than on a side street is learning a social studies concept as well as figuring out a mathematical pattern. And a child who notes that planes travel faster than trains travel faster than cars travel faster than bicycles travel faster than skateboards is picking up some science and technology while he makes a mathematical discovery.

Understanding Processes

"What's 20 plus 20?" a boy asks his grandfather.

"I'll show you how to figure that out," the grandfather answers. "Take off the zeroes. Then what do you have?"

"2 plus 2," says the child. "That's easy: 4."

"Now add the zero back."

"Both of them?"

"No. Just one."

"40?"

"That's right!"

Oh, thinks the child. But *why* is it 40?

For children to do well at anything, it's important for them to understand the process involved. Children in my school learn that they can solve pretty much any problem *in their own way,* by using a variety of concrete objects—counters, blocks, beads, and so on. But there's a big difference between understanding the process of something—what we need to figure out through experience—and understanding the procedure of something—what we can be taught.

- Process: what actually takes place between two numbers.
- Procedure: the steps required to determine (calculate) what takes place between these numbers.

Understanding that a process is inherent to the attainment of every goal is immeasurably valuable to a child and to the adults involved in a child's education. First and foremost, your child needs experience with concrete objects—counting them, sorting them, placing objects in a series, assessing them, and calculating with them. Then she needs to learn ways to represent the patterns she creates and the relationships she sees abstractly, through diagrams, graphs, numerals, and language. There's a natural progression from assigning forks to people at a table to counting forks, from building a block structure to building a Lego-block car from a diagram, from sorting clothes to take on a trip to writing "3 skirts + 3 shirts = 6 things in my suitcase." Understanding the true meaning of *number* and connecting it with symbols that are *numerals* comes in increments, through exploration, trial and error, support and affirmation.

Another note: some of you may have grown up studying "new math." Well, what we're doing today is *new* new math. The more educators learn about math, the more they see the value of bringing kids to the process, not the procedures, of math. The best schools are making sure the kids get the hands-on, nitty-gritty, do-and-discuss experiences they need. Eventually, children learn to see more sophisticated ways of doing math as shortcuts. Children who do things on the most basic level, then, can be proud of their math abilities enough to say, "I can add. I just didn't learn to write it yet." Or " . . . do it aloud" or ". . . do it in my head" or ". . . do it as fast as you." When you guide a child to see that there's a process in just about everything, he learns patience and confidence in his own ability to solve problems and move ahead.

Skills and Concepts

While much of the educational material on the market focuses on building specific skills, this book will instead help your child develop an understanding of needed concepts.

A *skill* is an activity that can be learned and that can improve with practice; for example, cutting with scissors, riding a tricycle, or printing numerals. A *concept,* on the other hand, is something that can't be taught directly. It's something each and every person comes to understand on his own. An example of a key concept in math is the idea of number. A very young child thinks that "three" is a word in a list much as "miny" is the third word in "eeny, meeny, miny, mo." As he grows he realizes that numbers aren't just part of a rhyme; they're meant to represent a quantity of things: red cars coming down the road, dolls on a shelf, potatoes in the pot. He's understanding a concept: that those words—"two," "three," "four"—stand for objects. Sure, you can *tell* him, but until he realizes that the words he says as he points are each connected to one object, he won't really *get* the concept of counting. Eventually he'll grasp it through experience, as he matches teacups to teddy bears, his socks to his feet, the covers of his books to the stories inside. He'll absorb other counting concepts, too: there are two in a pair of socks, one for each foot; the number of objects changes if you take some away; you can have *more* cookies than another child but not necessarily *the most*.

A child works with information by observing and doing. She takes the information in, ponders it, and comes up with her own personal hypothesis. But that's a simplistic way to describe the process. The acquisition of a concept happens over time. It fades in and out, becoming strong only after much experience.

This is not to say that children don't acquire skills through activities. Take Activity 23: Print 'n' Press, which involves using the different sides of blocks to create two-dimensional stamps with paint on paper. First, children experiment with stamping different sides of the blocks. Then they stamp the stamps in size order. This is a physical activity requiring *three-dimensional* objects to create a picture out of *two-dimensional* stamps. As such, it hits a lot of different concepts, but mainly drives home the idea that a mark on paper can represent a thing in the world. And the mark on the paper comes from the block. As the child moves ahead, she'll realize she doesn't need to stamp the whole block, she can just trace the block or draw it.

Sure, it might seem faster to just put it all on paper or to *tell* your child what the marks mean, guiding her eyes and hands, rather than letting her figure it out herself. But would it be the same? Would your child understand it? Would there be room for trial and error, design and discovery, me and you?

Every experience provided through the activities in this book will help your child develop concepts that will lead to a skilled understanding of math and a happy confidence in using it.

About the Activities

The activities in this book are chock-full of my philosophy of learning. They will help you create math experiences out of just about any situation, in and out of your home. They encompass chores, games, work, and play. The activities are organized into the following areas:

Part One: **Number Concepts**. These activities will help your child get a handle on numbers, numerals, counting, and calculation.

Part Two: **Space, Shape, and Measurement**. Here you'll find many ideas for helping your child understand how objects relate to one another and to the space around them. Key here is a development of understanding of how things come to be measured—through standard methods (like inches or centimeters and ounces or grams) and nonstandard methods of your child's invention.

Part Three: **Patterns and Relationships**. What comes next? What belongs? What doesn't belong? These activities involve observation, arrangement, and analysis.

Part Four: **Math Strategies**. This section is a smorgasbord of games and things to do to weave problem-solving strategies into everyday activities.

You don't have to pursue the activities in order. Jump around. Pick and choose. Generally, it's best to choose what appeals to you and to your child's interests, doing activities from each section, picking out what fits in with things you do already. Then change, adapt, mold the activity to make it your own.

For each activity, you'll see the following structure:

- **Name of Activity:** the title, followed by a few words telling what the activity is about, what its heart is
- **Helps Develop:** concepts and skills addressed
- **You'll Need:** a list of materials
- **Before You Begin:** actions to take and things to consider before starting
- **What to Do:** step-by-step directions
- **Follow-up Activities:** ways to redo and build on the activity in the future
- **What's Happening:** an explanation of what your child stands to gain from the activity as well as how it relates to school experience
- **Moving Ahead:** ways to take the activity to a higher level

- **Helpful Hint:** a word of advice or a reference to a helpful book or material

Each activity is labeled with the places you're most likely to use the activities: around the house, out and about (market, mall, library, pool), close to home (yard, garden, park, street, woods) and from here to there (in transit, public or private).

How You Can Get the Most Out of the Activities

Understand Your Child's Development

"My child can count to 13." ". . . to 19." ". . . to 45."

"My child's already adding." ". . . subtracting." ". . . dividing."

Any time two parents sit around talking about their children, somebody's likely to go home anxious. But understanding and accepting your child's level of mathematical development will help calm that quavering heart. Part of the great division (if you will) that exists between people who love math and people who hate math comes from wrong notions about what constitutes math learning. Division is something you get at the end of third grade, right? Multiplication tables are something you know cold by fifth grade, eh?

I'm here to tell you a few things that may seem contradictory: First, counting, by itself, without reference to objects, is no more an indication of an understanding of numbers than reciting the alphabet is an indication of being able to read. Second, children can always do more than they can say. A child of two or three has the basic *concepts* of addition and subtraction, multiplication and division firmly in hand. If you don't believe me, just try to give him two cookies while giving his friend three.

What's more, your child today will be different from your child yesterday. Still, you wonder whether he's growing fast enough, far enough, soon enough. Some educators will attempt to tell you and may even place your child on a chart to show you where he is in terms of development and how he compares with other kids. But I find a child's position impossible to pinpoint scientifically.

Kids develop at different rates physically. Look at all the shapes and sizes of your child's playmates. Well, rates of emotional, social, and intellectual development are as diverse as rates of physical development. Celebrate how interesting your child's development is, rather than worry about it. "How?" you ask. Here are a few basic tips:

- **Don't push.** When your previously independent child counts on her fingers, let her. Hug that kid. Praise her for solving a problem in her own way with the materials at hand (literally). Don't protest, inwardly or outwardly.

- **Don't compare.** "Comparisons are odious," said a poet. They are not needed in formal education, and certainly not in the kind of informal education that is the premise of this book.

- **Don't be overly concerned about testing.** Some schools will tell you that they use tests to determine something called "mental age" as opposed to physical or chronological age. The score is often based on a brief interview between your child and a total stranger, some questions, and an assessment that places your child on a continuum with others of the same chronological age. Research has *not* documented the validity of such testing for predicting future "success" in school. No test can judge a child's motivation to learn, enthusiasm about school, ability to reason and solve problems in a variety of situations. These kinds of tests are based on comparisons among children. They judge a child on a specific day, in an artificial setting, and using questions that are often meaningless to the child. Even worse, such testing has been shown to influence how parents and teachers treat a child. This can ultimately harm the child's self-esteem.

Accept Your Child's Developmental Level and Interests

"He's really very intelligent," one father told me. "But when I tell him I'll read to him when he's got his pajamas on, brushed his teeth, and hung up his towel, he comes to me in his pajamas, teeth unbrushed. So I say, 'Go back and brush your teeth and hang up your towel.' He goes and brushes his teeth. Then I have to send him back to hang up the towel! What's his problem? "

"No problem," I said. "That's just where he is in life."

This father was asking his child to come read a story after he'd done three things. That's as complicated a request as saying, "Go find me the red book with the black lettering that's on the counter." To a child, that's too much to consider. A young child can consider one attribute: she focuses on that one and barely hears the rest. She'll bring you a red book, but it might not be the one you asked for.

If you really want that child to be ready for his story, give him one thing at a time to do. Understand that it's not a matter of remembering a list of instructions so much as understanding different factors, characteristics, and attributes. And help him grow at his own pace. If you can understand that he can handle just one attribute at a time, you will say, "Get your pajamas on. Done? Okay, toothbrushing time." Keep it to one or two attributes until you're sure he can handle more: "Okay, if you've got your pajamas on and brushed your teeth, you can have a story."

The point is this: if you can accept that your child is on the road to somewhere, at a step in the process of learning, then you won't have to worry that he's going nowhere. Above all, be interested and receptive every time your child has anything to do with math— even something that seems as tangential as ready-for-bed instructions. Practice, experience, and encouraging language will lead him on.

Acknowledge Your Child's Abilities

If acceptance is about attitude, acknowledgment is about observation and words to go with it. True math understanding relies first on experience, second on visual observation, and third on using language to express what is experienced and observed.

When you're doing math activities with your child, make statements that express and describe what she's doing without criticism or overgeneral praise. Say your child suggests that she has more peas than her brother because her peas are more spread out on her plate. Say, "Why don't you line them up, one for one," not "Just because they're positioned differently, that doesn't mean there are more."

When you're talking with your child, acceptance is asking questions that are open-ended and nonjudgmental. Say you're trying to help your child gain practice in experiences that lead to one-to-one correspondence. Ask, "Can you put one egg in each cup?" not "How many eggs are there?" The point is not to challenge your child but to engage her interest in an activity that will lead to better understanding. Discuss the activity in a way that leads to more discussion: rather than saying, "Hey, great! You filled all the cups!," make an observation. "Hmm, this cup has an egg, and this, and this. No empty cups at all? What about leftover eggs? Just one?"

Also, and this is *important*, let your child draw her own conclusions: she may not realize, because of her stage of development, that having a leftover egg means that there were more eggs than cups to start with. One characteristic of this age group is that they make assumptions that aren't logical to adults. For example, young children *really think* that if you spread out your peas, you have more than you do if you bunch them together. You can't get them to get it (*it*, in this case, being the concept of conservation) by telling them. Rather, you have to give them more and more experience by encouraging them to enjoy whatever they're doing—sorting, arranging, matching, looking at, and talking about.

Give Your Child's Math Résumé Muscle

Math has a lot of tricky concepts that can really boggle your mind, whether you're a child or an adult. Every adult can probably recall sitting and staring at one math problem while the mind remained blank, waiting for the proverbial lightbulb to go on. For each of us to deal with math, we need experiences of different kinds. Here are some of the vital ones that you can give your child:

Make things with your child. Some of the activities in this book rely on materials that need to be bought or made. My advice in almost every situation is to make them yourself. Take number rods, for instance. To make them, you're going to take a long rod and saw it up. Your child is going to help you measure the 1-inch piece, the 2-inch piece, and so on up to the 10-inch piece. She's going to help you saw them, sand them, and paint them. Who's going to have a deeper understanding of the relationship between those rods: your child or the child who comes over to visit and plays with the rods?

Play games with your child. Consider the procedures you go through to play a particular game, the concepts you need to understand to play it (addition? matching? classification?), the protocol, the dexterity you need to hold your hand of cards or move cards around on the table, the strategy and sportsmanship that must be learned, and, of course, the enjoyment you and your child share in this activity, which is so much more than math. One educator I know makes playing card games the center of her math curriculum. Playing cards have number values, numerals, symbols, colors, pictures, front and back, and patterns of all kinds. Other games have their own inherent concepts, procedures, and protocols. Mancala (Activity 51) involves just about every key concept area. Checkers involves area, pattern, and strategy. Monopoly is tied in with sorting, classifying, matching, counting, figuring out currency, and even moving along a board that has sides exactly ten places long.

Diagram activities with your child. As often as possible, engage your child in re-creating an activity on paper. Some of the activities in this book deal with this directly, but almost all can be used as material for recording or diagraming. Say your child has six eggs and five cups. After he has spent some time matching them up, suggest that he draw a picture showing what he did. He'll be translating from the three-dimensional plane to a two-dimensional piece of paper.

Take turns with your child at giving and following directions. You might have your child direct you to replicate his actions with the eggs and cups. He'll get experience this time in translating actions into words. You might try taking down his directions on a piece of paper to show him how they look step-by-step. And let him follow your directions, going from words to action.

Boost Your Child's Confidence

Who's in charge? When it comes to your child's work, the answer, of course, is your child. Approach any activity—building, or playing a game, or baking a cake—as if you were a master working with an apprentice. Your role is not to be a boss, but a guide. Here are some encouraging phrases you can use:

"Hey! You figured out a new way to put your toy cars in order! What's the pattern?"

"I don't know how tall the Statue of Liberty is. How do you think we can find out?"

"I know one way to fold this paper in half. Can you think of another way?"

"This building is really tall. How did you get it to stay up?"

"I'm following your diagram, but I can't figure out what to do next. Can you give me a tip?"

Notice that you're not giving answers or suggesting ways to find them, but suggesting *finding* ways to find them. You're suggesting a goal and opening the discussion up to ways to meet the goal, rather than instructing. And you're encouraging with words that describe, not judge: *tall* rather than *impressive* or *good*. And, always, you're asking questions that recognize that your child has ideas or explanations of the subject at hand.

Explore, Explain, Discuss

As much as possible, discuss every situation that involves math with your child. This may mean explaining the purpose of a check or credit card, figuring out how far it is to the nearest crosswalk, or marking the calendar for the dog's next heartworm pill. Explain what's happening, why it's happening, and how to figure it out.

By doing this, you make visible to your child your thought processes as you consider a real-life math problem, and you encourage her to discuss her own with you. Again and again and again, get her talking about what she's doing with her hands and what she's thinking as she does it.

Each activity in this book can be introduced through a question: "I wonder . . . ?" "What if . . . ?" "How . . . ?" Open-ended questions require you to be less of an expert. Open-ended questions require your child to become more of an explorer.

The key action is to use an everyday situation, ask an "I wonder . . . " question, and open it to the child to find out or to figure out. I'm certainly not into scripting interactions, but here are a few examples:

"I wonder how many different ways there are to take the crayons out of the box in twos?"

"What if we wanted to make a double batch of cookies?"

"How can we measure this room?"

"Look at this floor full of cars. I wonder which ones go together."

Listen to your child. Look at your child. Watch what she does. You can't find out whether a child understands how to group a big pile of objects by asking her. Children can always *do* more than they can *explain*.

Talk through your processes, explaining how you do what you do and why you do it that way. Without this experience, children just see the end product and think, "You're perfect. You decide to do something and you do it, magically." That's how it can appear. Most of our everyday processing is invisible to children. Become more verbal about what you're planning, thinking, doing. "See, I'm drawing this diagram of your bedroom. I'm trying to decide if the hamper will go better next to the closet or at the foot of your bed. If I put it by the door, I think it will get in the way. Each of these little squares stands for a space about this big [spread hands a foot apart]. Where else could the hamper go? You figured out a new way! Great! Let's go try all the ways, and see which one you think works best."

Getting Your Child Started with Math

So you want to get your child started? If your child is already born, then you *have* already started, through the atmosphere you've created in your home. When children are involved in building, counting, measuring, and doing other real-life, everyday math activities, they learn that math is a natural part of life. Families foster math awareness at home by gathering an assortment of interesting goods, encouraging experimentation and discussion, setting up many interesting situations, playing games, and suggesting pencil-and-paper activities at appropriate times. The atmosphere in these homes is what I call a math stew.

The best stews are the ones that take a long time, that start in the morning with a bone and some water and simmer all day, with new ingredients added as the day goes on: herbs, wine, vegetables. What I wish for all children is that they might grow up sloshing around in a math stew in their homes.

You can create a math stew for your child out of all the objects—things you might not typically think of as math materials—around the house. Here are just a few of the "ingredients" your child will benefit from: newspapers, grocery circulars, junk drawers, bath toys, wood scraps, seashells, dominoes, pots and pans, cloth napkins, suitcases, rocks, paper dolls, modeling dough, containers, movable numbers, playing cards, things in different sizes, paper, crayons, counters (beads or bingo chips, for example), a calculator, a clock, a scale, and anything else that comes into the house that involves math. You'll also need books that have to do with numbers: counting, shape-finding, and so on. (For more specific suggestions, see the activities.)

But math is more than just looking, it's doing. Do the activities in this book, and involve your child in your own math activities. Let him see you doing math: following diagrams, measuring, balancing your checkbook, doubling recipes, trying a 60-watt bulb in place of a 100-watt bulb, planning a dinner party. Tell him what you're doing and why you're doing it. Do it with him. And know when to back off and let him do his own explorations, repetitions, and investigations.

There's another vital ingredient. It's free, requires no construction or assembly, and is readily available. It's talk. When they say talk is cheap, they're underestimating its value. If a child is going to be able to analyze patterns, identify relationships, and make generalizations, he's going to have to be able to put his observations and actions into words. One of my favorite sayings is "I can name what I can do; I can do what I can name." Still, many of the "math kids" I know spend considerable time simply observing, processing, analyzing, drawing conclusions based on their experiences. For them, talk takes a back seat to the mental gears that really drive the math car.

Finally, stir in some math attitude. Be positive, excited, fascinated about what you and your child are doing together. But what if you're not good at math? What if you *hate* math? What if you can't even balance your checkbook? Relax. You're not alone. Many of us can't. (It's not real math anyway; it's arithmetic.) It's essential to get rid of the notion that you're not good in math. You *are* good in math. People who say they can't write are often talking about grammar, punctuation, and spelling—areas their teachers red-lined back in high school. People who say they're bad at math are often talking about computation. But if you can figure out which bag or bowl to put the leftovers in, you're good at math. If you can estimate how long it's going to take you to travel to your nearest national park, you're good at math. If you can get all the different parts of a meal ready at the same time, you're exceptional at math. And if you can program your VCR, you can come to my house and do mine. (I'm not going to tell you you're spectacular at math if you can do that; rather, you're good at following cryptic directions, a different kind of skill.)

Put away those notions of being good or bad at math. Don't waste time trying to figure out if your child is good or bad at math. Instead, dive—both of you—into the math stew. Play, experiment, draw, diagram, talk, and describe. You'll dispel your own math nightmares and help make your child's math life a dream.

Choosing the Best Materials

This stew—like any good stew—doesn't require a major financial investment. Sure, you could go to your favorite educational toy catalog and order up a storm, but this is unnecessary, and expensive. Rather, make a point of choosing quality toys that can be used in many ways. By quality toys, I don't necessarily mean items that your cool kid won't fall in love with. You'll want to have something that has many possibilities for exploration, discussion, drama, sorting, and manipulating. These could be baskets of wooden fruit made in Italy or the collections of Barbies or Batmen that you may already have lying around the house.

Here are some guidelines for choosing math materials for you and your child:

- Choose materials that appeal to *both* you and your child.

Your child's going to use them over and over—and so may you.

- Find some groups of simple materials that are the same except for one characteristic or attribute:

      a bunch of little cars in different colors

      blocks of the same shape in different sizes

      white envelopes in different shapes

- Find some materials that have several different attributes: anything from action figures to pots and pans.

- Look for durable goods that have multiple uses: for counting, sorting, classifying, or building.

- Make your own math materials (such as number rods, shape stamps, and bead counters) with your child. The purpose of the material will become evident through the process of making it into something else. Your child will gain in motor skills through making something, and he will gain in the understanding of process through following steps with you.

- Include drawing and writing materials as part of your essential math supplies. The abilities to diagram and to write about math are covered much too little in many classrooms and are necessary to true math understanding, as well as to the word problems, geometry proofs, and SAT questions that will come later.

- Use your library to the hilt! Librarians can point you toward math picture books. Library collections may include math toys that can be borrowed.

- There's only one item you can't do without: blocks. I recommend wooden ones of varying sizes, plain wood or painted—it doesn't matter which. Make your own, or buy them. As your child grows, add Lincoln Logs, which fit together like log cabins, or Kapla blocks, which are flat and stackable, or connecting blocks like Duplo and Lego, or Mottik, a construction toy with triangles, squares, and wheels that join together. A word of caution: don't assume that because your child's school has blocks, she's getting ample experience there. Research shows that boys and girls stake out different areas of nursery schools, and that boys generally rule the block area. Even if teachers strive to change this, girls seem to end up spending less time with the blocks. Have your own set at home, play with your child, give her every chance to get all that good stuff that blocks bring.

Jumping-Off Point

A college student was frustrated with her classes, beginning-level psychology, philosophy, economics, and sociology. "It's all stuff everybody knows anyway!" she complained. "It's fancy names for how people think, whether the world exists, how people make money, and why your friends are your friends. So what?"

"Sure," I said, "But did you ever really think about them before? Did you ever read about them, talk about them, study them?"

Math classes at the college level cause a different sort of complaint. Nobody expects to already know anything they learn there. They're sometimes surprised, though. Not your child. Start now, and your child will have a clear understanding through life that math is part of what "everybody knows anyway."

Ask some questions. You'll be amazed by what she already knows.

> *Q.* What's the difference between a ball and a block?
>
> *A.* A ball is squooshy, and a block is hard. One is wooden and the other isn't. One has corners and the other has a round circle.
>
> —Emily, age 5

> *Q.* Which is faster, a dog or a skateboard?
>
> *A.* It depends. It depends on whether the dog is walking or running and if the skateboard is going fast or slow. If the dog was walking, then the skateboard is going faster, but if the dog was running, then there's a good chance that the dog could be faster. If the dog was on a leash, then he would probably be walking, because his owner would be with him. But if his owner was on a skateboard and the dog was pulling him, then that would be awesome. The dog generally would be faster because he's in front, pulling it.
>
> —Sam, age 6½

A child will learn math in his own way. For me, it's fabulous to watch it happen over and over with each different child, in so many different ways. The key is to accept what the child is doing, on his level. Nobody says to a child who has taken a step, "That's not walking. Here, look at your brother. Now, that's walking."

In the same way, a child who is rolling marbles into each other or standing books up in tent shapes (rather than reading them) is on his way to math understanding. He's messing around, watching what happens, seeing patterns, making generalizations. When adults accept a child's math explorations on his level—three-year-old, six-year-old, twelve-year-old, and so on—and focus instead on the discoveries being made, then the child grows in confidence, takes more risks, uses math more fully, and communicates his understanding—soon enough—on the adult level. And his life, and the adults', will be richer for it.

"Look what I built!"

"Hey, I'm taller than the counter."

"I wrote all these numbers."

"Want to know how many eggs are left?"

Strive to create an atmosphere that accepts every answer and leaves the way open for new thought, new experiments, new answers, so that your child's joyful, confident math exploration will never end.

PART ONE

Basic Mathematical Concepts

The emphasis in this section is on concrete experiences, three-dimensional materials, and open explorations that will enhance your child's ability to count and compute. The ability to count relies on a firm foundation of one-to-one correspondence, seriation (placing things in a series), understanding of numbers as numerals, and experience with conservation (a number of items stays the same no matter how the items are arranged).

The section starts out very simply and moves on to higher-level concepts and skills. Just about every math experience in this book involves some counting, conserving, and understanding relationships. For the best possible experience, combine these activities with those in the other sections.

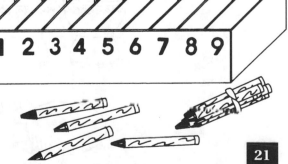

1 Eggs to Cups

This classic activity will help you understand your child's level of understanding of one-to-one correspondence. Remember that no amount of discussion or explanation will change a child's understanding of this concept. Only experience with numbers and objects will bring her forward.

Helps develop: one-to-one correspondence, matching, constancy of numbers

You'll Need   6 egg cups or small cups; 8 to 10 wooden or plastic toy eggs

Before You Begin   For this activity, you'll set some egg cups in a line, and place some eggs to the side.

What to Do
1. Show your child the egg cups and eggs. Ask her to pick out enough eggs so that there will be one egg for each egg cup.

2 Watch what your child does and talk to her about how she figures out how many eggs to pick out. "Oh, I see, you're putting an egg in each cup," or "How did you figure it out?"

Follow-up Activities
- Ask your child to put the eggs back to the side and to line up a different number of egg cups for you to assign eggs to. Ask your child to walk you through the procedure she used to figure out how many eggs are needed.

- Get your child involved in a variety of matching (one-to-one correspondence) activities, from planting seeds in holes to assigning toy cars to garages, paintbrushes to paint jars, straws to cups, spoons to bowls, or hats to heads.

The Swiss behaviorist Jean Piaget, whose research forms the basis of much modern thought about children's development, used this activity to learn how math understanding develops in young children. He concluded that very young children could not solve this problem at all at first. At the second stage of development (roughly ages four to seven), children would match one egg to each cup to arrive at the right total. Matching is the foundation of the concept of one-to-one correspondence—an important step on the road to learning to count.

Moving Ahead Put your empty egg cups in a row. Lay the same number of eggs end to end in front of the cups so that they form a longer row than the cups. Ask your child what there's more of: eggs or cups. Most likely a child in the age group four to seven will answer that there are more eggs—even if she has just seen that there is one egg for each cup. To her the row of eggs is longer; therefore it has more. Don't discuss it. Just let her play with the eggs. Through experience in matching eggs to cups, she'll realize eventually that the number of eggs remains the same no matter how the eggs are arranged.

Helpful Hint More matching activities:

- Ask your child to make signs for every bedroom, chair, or coat hook, using a picture or name as the label.
- Ask your child to distribute a bunch of flowers among several vases. Explore the various ways there are to do this: one-to-one, two-to-one, all in one and none in the others, two in one and three in the others, and so on.
- Play cards with your child and ask her to deal a certain number of cards per person. Try Activity 50: Poker Faces, or Activity 53: Go Fish!

2 Family Pictures

Helps develop:
ordering,
seriation, understand-
ing of graphing

*Will everyone please line up
from the shortest to the tallest?*

You'll Need

butcher paper; pencils; paper for labels; scissors; glue or paste; collage material such as wallpaper, wrapping paper, yarn, pipe cleaners, and buttons or plastic googly eyes for eyes; poster board

Before You Begin

Explore the notion of comparative size with your child by asking open-ended questions about objects: "Hmm. I wonder if any of these rocks is bigger than the others." "Which of these pencils seems longer?"

What to Do

1 Talk with your child about the height of each of your family members. Who's the tallest? The shortest?

2 Help your child rank the family in order from shortest to tallest. Don't write this down—just say it aloud.

3 Tell your child that you have an idea of a way to show the height ranking on paper. "What if we made a model of each person?"

4 Starting with the shortest person, trace a life-size model of each family member on butcher paper. Now ask your child to use labels to describe the figures in order of size. Write each label on the appropriate paper. Labels might read, "This is Alana"; then, "This is Kerrie. She is taller than Alana." And so on, up to the tallest person.

Follow-up Activities

• Discuss what makes one thing bigger or taller than another.

• Invite your child to use collage materials to paste models of each family member on a large sheet of paper or poster board with the shortest at the lower left, and each successively taller model going to the right.

• Encourage your child to create other graphs depicting toys or dolls that he owns.

What's Happening   Your child has taken a look at his family members, figured out their size order, and re-created the situation in art work. By doing so, he figured out through experience just what it is that makes one person taller than another: longer legs, for one thing. In addition, he created a basic form of a graph, a common tool for showing relationships symbolically. By simply representing real people two-dimensionally, your child moves closer to truly graphic representation.

Moving Ahead   Create a graph of *The Three Bears*. Use collage materials to create (on a large sheet of poster board) a big Papa Bear, smaller Mama Bear, and smallest Baby Bear, across the top of the paper. Below each of them, create a bowl, a chair, and a bed that correspond in size to that bear.

Helpful Hint   One of the simplest graphs around is created in many homes by families who mark their heights on a doorway. Assign a different color pencil to each person—including adults—and use the same color each time you mark that person's height. Children will be able to see at a glance their own growth—and that adult size remains constant.

3 The Book of Four

*"'For two can stick together,' said Pooh, said he,
'That's how it is,' said Pooh."*

from Now We Are Six *by A. A. Milne*

You'll Need construction paper; stapler *or* needle and heavy thread; crayons

Before You Begin Do a little counting with your child to determine how high she can comfortably count. The reason I've named this activity "The Book of Four" is that four is less than five, a number that serves as a sort of benchmark for counting accuracy. If your child is able to count five or more of something from a pile, you can make this a book of five or higher. A younger child will more likely benefit from doing this book with the numbers one to four. Note that your child will not benefit from your upping the number in hope of pressing him forward.

What to Do
1 Fold several sheets of construction paper in half, and put the folds together to form a book. Staple or sew the edge to hold the book together.

2 Title your book "The Book of Four" or whatever your number is. Write the numeral 4 on the cover along with the title.

3 Invite your child to look for things that come in fours: horses' legs, car wheels, chair legs, and others. Suggest that your child use each page of the book to draw one of these fours and write (in invented writing) a caption for the drawing.

4 Ask your child to read her book to you.

Follow-up Activities
• Be on the lookout for things that come in fours in the grocery store, playground, and other places. Ask your child to draw these things. Add pages to the book or suggest that your child fill some that may have been left blank.

• Suggest another book about another number.

When they are very young, children gain an understanding of the essence of numbers: "the twoness of two"—me and you, Piglet and Pooh—and "the threeness of three." Their ability to count to higher numbers is no indication that they understand them in this way. Practical experience is helpful to move children along into understandings of four, five, and higher numbers.

Moving Ahead

Give your child plenty of practical experience with counting out objects in fours. One excellent way to do this is the card game Go Fish. A young child can learn the principles of the game by making pairs the goal. Let an older child fish for tricks—all four cards of a denomination. See Activity 53: Go Fish!

Helpful Hint

As your child counts objects, have her move them to one side, one by one. Placing a finger on each object is helpful, too, but children may count objects randomly and forget what's already been counted, unless they physically move them.

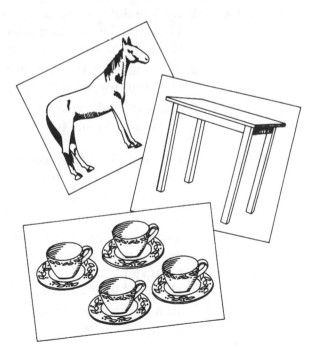

4 Giant Dot to Dot

This variation on the theme of hopscotch turns a longtime favorite activity into a game your child can touch, change, and move through.

You'll Need permanent marker; dots: old coasters, screw-on lids from jars, plastic lids from margarine containers, rubber lid grippers, or any other flat object 3 to 5 inches (6 to 10 cm) in diameter, substantial enough not to blow away: you can even use rocks if you have enough available

Before You Begin Number the dots from 1 to 10. Use higher numbers as your child progresses.

What to Do

1 Lay the dots out on the ground for your child to follow. They may be one step apart, or far enough apart that your child has to walk from one to another.

2 Ask your child to follow the dots in numerical order, jumping, stepping, or walking from one to the next.

3 Ask your child to lay the dots out for you. Take your turn moving from one to the next, counting aloud, in order.

Follow-up Activities

• Ask your child to follow the dots backward. Have him move backward if he wants!

• Lay all the dots out very close together. Ask your child to step only on the even or odd numbers.

• Ask your child to do something special when he moves to a certain number: cha-cha from even to odd numbers, take giant steps from odd to even; or jump over every dot whose number has the syllable -*teen* in it.

• Toss all the dots out randomly. Challenge your child to go from one to the next in order despite the jumble.

What's Happening Accurate counting is the ability to match one numeral to one object and to use the numerals in correct sequence. This game allows your child opportunities to physically move through the counting process, and to see and experience numerals in many ways.

Moving Ahead Take some chalk and your dots and find an empty sidewalk or parking lot. Before or after your child walks or jumps from dot to dot, have him chalk the path he must take. Then move the markers into another pattern. Chalk this path. When you've played a few times, check out the variety in the paths and compare the patterns.

Helpful Hint Hopscotch is very instructive, because it requires drawing shapes with numbers inside. To draw a good hopscotch board, a child has to assess foot size, jump length, and so on. You can also make a giant indoor version of hopscotch by cutting shapes from carpet scraps (don't use cardboard; it'll slip on the floor), numbering them with markers, and having your child jump from one shape to the next.

5 Easy as 1, 2, 3

One, two, buckle my shoe,
Three, four, shut the door,
Five, six, pick up sticks,
Seven, eight, lay them straight,
Nine, ten, a big fat hen.

You'll Need edible counters: peanuts, M&M's, grapes, goldfish crackers, or raisins; glue; cardboard; pencil

Before You Begin Give your child experience with naming numerals, as in the nursery rhyme above. This will help her know in what order to give numerals as she's counting the number of things.

What to Do

1 Set a container of your counters between you and your child. Casually ask her to pass you a small number—three or four—of them. If she counts as she passes, fine. If she passes them one by one without speaking, you count as she hands you each one.

2 Now ask for two more. Say, "Hmm, I wonder how many I have now?" Count the total with your child.

3 Ask your child, "How many would you like?" Have her count them out herself, or count them with her.

4 Decide which of your snacks you'll eat first, next, and so on, and encourage your child to do the same. Suggest that your child line up her snacks in order of eating. Say things like "Which one are you going to eat next?" "I only have three left," and "I'm going to eat two together."

5 When they're all gone, call it quits. Or set some more, and do it again!

Follow-up Activities

• Arrange the counters into a group of ten. A big bag of colored candies is great for this, because every time you count out ten, you'll get a different combination of colors. Also organize the ten candies by color.

• Divide your candies into ones and twos as in the following diagram. Do the first three or four, then ask your child to finish the pattern. This helps your child see odds and evens.

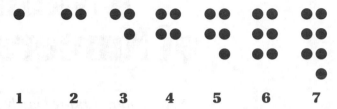

| 1 | 2 | 3 | 4 | 5 | 6 | 7 |

- Paste your snacks onto a sheet of cardboard and write numerals beside each of them. If your child balks at this, suggest tracing them—a highly motivational next level to the activity that lets her have her snack and eat it too.

What's Happening

Parents often think that children can count because they can say numerals in order. Real counting comes when a child assigns each object a numeral and recognizes that a numeral stands for the amount represented. Basic understanding of number begins in babyhood, when a child learns to see herself as one, to see her arms and legs and ears and eyes as twos, and so on. After the number three, number concept comes through experience with arranging and rearranging objects.

This activity helps you provide several kinds of experiences. Make it a regular activity and you'll help your child see that one group of objects can be used to represent many different numbers in different groupings. Note that knowledge of numerals is also key. Your child does need to know the sound and order of numbers—something easily taught through nursery rhymes.

Moving Ahead
- Ask your child to divide a bag of snacks among four people.
- Ask your child to make a line of snacks from one end of the table to the other. Ask her to predict how many it will take.

Helpful Hint
Play Mancala (Activity 51), substituting snacks for beans. Eat your winnings!

6 A Number of Numerals

*Helps develop:
purpose of numerals, writing numerals, linking numerals with number, one-to-one correspondence*

Natural numbers are loosely defined as amounts of objects in real life that can be accounted for, seen, experienced. Negative numbers aren't natural numbers, because they can't be seen. Young children usually have a good concept of natural numbers up to about four: the number of legs on the cat, say. This activity will help your child see the numerals 1 through 9 as figures that stand for natural numbers.

You'll Need
sandpaper; small box, such as a shoebox; counters: beans, checkers, crayons, and so on; paper; scissors; crayons or markers; magnet numerals

Before You Begin
Cut the shapes of the numerals 1 to 9 from sandpaper. Make each numeral 2 inches (5 cm) tall or taller, and place the numerals in the box.

What to Do
1 Start with the numeral 1. Ask your child to take it out of the box and examine it.

2 Talk about how the 1 is shaped, and how it feels to the touch.

3 Talk about how one of something looks. Invite your child to take one counter and place it beside the numeral 1.

4 Move on to the 2 and to the other numerals in the same manner. With a very young child, stop at the 4 or the 5. Let him explore the rest of the numerals and the counters through play. If your child seems interested and able to match numeral and quantity, move ahead.

Follow-up Activities
• Invite your child to use the sandpaper numerals as tracing templates. Beside the traced numeral, he can glue or draw an appropriate number of counters. See Activity 3: The Book of Four.

• Ask your child to find the matching numeral in a selection of magnet numerals.

Too much in standard mathematics education is about looking. Children should be encouraged to get to know numerals—as well as the numbers they represent—with their hands. Numerals, like letters, don't make sense on their own to children. Numerals need to be linked to numbers through sensory connections, just as letters need to be read as words ("bee," "dee," "ess") to make sense to a child.

Moving Ahead

Cut the symbols +, –, and = out of sandpaper. Once your child is accustomed to counting counters to see what the number is when you have three and add two more, you can introduce symbols that show the relationship. See Activity 14: Add In, Take Out.

Helpful Hint

Take a walk with your child and look for numerals. Talk about each one you see and discuss its meaning.

7 Making a Bundle

This large-scale game lets your child get her hands on the individual items that make up a group and the group that each numeral represents.

Helps develop: one-to-one correspondence, understanding of volume and weight

You'll Need a large cardboard box lid fitted with cardboard dividers to make ten compartments that are at least 7 by 3 inches (18 by 8 cm); 55 crayons; stick-on numbers from a stationery or hardware store; rubber bands

Before You Begin Make a box with compartments to look like the one in the picture. Do this by cutting lengths of cardboard (the same length as the box) and taping them firmly to the bottom and ends of the box to hold them in place.

What to Do

1 Use the stick-on numbers to label each compartment, from left to right, 0 to 9.

2 Ask your child to help you count out the number of crayons that belongs in each compartment. Do not count them in one at a time; rather, for the "2" compartment, count two, and say, "This is a two." Then bundle them together with a rubber band, and place the bundle in the compartment.

3 Use these crayons as the starting point for activities requiring addition, subtraction, and understanding of more, less, and equal. For example, have your child take out the bundle of five. Ask her, "How else can you make five?" Your child may suggest taking one away from the 6 bundle or putting the 3 bundle and the 2 bundle together.

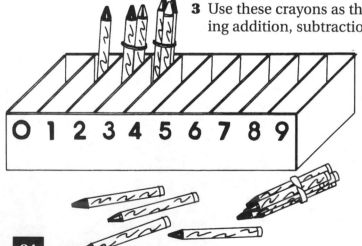

Follow-up Activity   Use the bundles of crayons to measure weight by feeling in Activity 18: Sock Scale.

What's Happening   *Your child can see the numeral on each compartment. She can also see the crayons in the compartments, of a number to match the numeral. This marriage of number and representational numeral is key.*

Another outcome of this activity is the child's growth in understanding that a number is made up of equal parts. The child learns about weight as she handles the crayons, bundles them together, and compares the heft of, say, 5 as opposed to 4. By fitting the crayons into compartments of equal size, the child observes how 1 fits in, how 9 fits in, and gains understanding of the relationship between number and volume. Finally this activity helps a child to understand the reversible nature of arithmetic functions: If you have nine crayons and take away three, you have six left; if you add three back, you get nine again.

Moving Ahead   Early conceptual understanding of multiplication and division can be developed through questions such as "I wonder how many 2s you need to get 8?"

Helpful Hint   Use your bundle box as a receptacle for other items of a uniform shape and size: poker chips, marbles, and so on. Have your child work with these materials and compare them to the crayons.

35

8 Visit the Banker

Helps develop:
*basic computation,
understanding of number and place value*

"That'll be 1,000 beans, ma'am."

You'll Need many tiny things such as rice, beans, pebbles, or pennies (you'll need literally hundreds); small plastic bags and ties; transparent plastic bread bags and ties; stick-on paper labels; paper cups

Before You Begin Do this activity as an outgrowth of your child's invented play of store, post office, or other places of business in which goods are bought. This activity will allow you to create a money system of beans.

What to Do

1 Tell your child that you need his help to create a system of money to pay for things at his store. Everything will cost different amounts of beans, just as everything in real life costs different amounts of pennies.

2 Set up your system as follows:

- A plastic cup holds one to nine beans. If you place ten beans in the cup, exchange it for one small bag.

- Small plastic bags each hold ten beans. If you have ten small bags (100 beans), exchange it for one large bag

- Large plastic bags each hold ten small plastic bags of ten beans (100 beans in all).

3 Label each small bag with a sticker that says 10, each large bag with a sticker that says 100.

4 Set up the bank near the store. Ask your child to be banker. Write him a check by writing a number on a slip of paper (for example, *146*), and ask the banker to cash it, giving you the necessary number of hundreds, tens, and ones.

Follow-up Activity   Create a store with your child. Use your currency to buy and sell things there.

What's Happening   Using currency of any kind to buy something is a valuable lesson. Your child will easily move from fluency with this activity to understanding two- and three-digit numbers and will add to the foundation he needs to understand any system of currency. Of even more value is the experience your child will gain with using actual numbers of objects.

Moving Ahead   Ask your child to give you two or more numbers to add. Take the first number out of the bank, then take the second number out separately. How many hundreds all together? How many tens and ones? Ask your child (the banker) to let you know when you need to trade up from ones to tens, from tens to hundreds. Use your bank to build concepts of subtraction (what do you get if you take away?), multiplication (how many tens do I need to make a hundred?), and division (how many tens are in a hundred?).

Helpful Hint   You really need a lot of beans (or any other objects you like) to make this activity worthwhile. Most children will want the capability of going up to 1000! Use a hole punch to create confetti dots, or buy a huge bag of rice or beans from a price club.

9 Getting It on Tape

Helps develop: counting, understanding places, and one-to-one correspondence

*If your child laid all the numbers
from one end to the other,
they'd never ever stop going around the world.*

You'll Need adding machine tape; pencil; thin wooden dowel or stick (optional)

Before You Begin Prepare this activity when your child has become fairly adept at writing numerals and counting up to 100.

What to Do 1 Unroll about two feet of the adding machine tape. Give the child the end of the tape and a pencil. Invite him to write numerals on the tape, beginning in the bottom right corner of the tape with the numeral 1. This is so the numbers will fall into columns according to place as the child moves up to two- and three-digit numbers.

2 Encourage your child to continue writing numerals in order in this way until she wants to stop.

Follow-up Activity Try Activity 10: Places, Everyone!

It's necessary for the numeral 1 to fall in the bottom right corner so that numbers written above it fall into columns of ones, tens, and hundreds. There's a pattern to the writing of numbers, and children who practice writing numbers in this way will grasp that pattern. You'll know it's happening when you see your child begin to fill in the ones column by just writing 1, 2, 3, and so on, and then going back to fill in the tens column with all 1s (for 10, 11, 12, 13, and so on). For this reason, let your child repeatedly write 1 to 100 if she wants. She'll cement the pattern in her mind, moving up in good time when she's ready. Why write from the bottom up? This reinforces the notion that higher numbers stand for larger amounts.

Moving Ahead

This activity is long-lasting. (My grandson has a roll whose diameter is bigger than my hand.) The next time your child wants to do this activity, she may want to continue the tape she started, or she may want to start all over again. Leave the decision to her.

Helpful Hint

Display the tape in one of the following ways. Hang it in a place where your child can look at it: above the eating table, above her bed, on the bathroom wall. She'll gain practice reading numerals and will pick up some patterns that she might not have noted while writing.

- Hang from the top end.
- Roll the tape back up for future additions.
- Roll the tape over a dowel long enough to hold several tapes and hang the dowel.

10 Places, Everyone!

Everyone!

Helps develop:
*understanding
of number, place value,
basic arithmetic
functions and
computation*

Numbers: how do they stack up?

You'll Need

medium-weight cardboard; ruler; marking pen; pencil; counters such as pennies, bingo chips, or popcorn kernels

Before You Begin

This activity is for children who have the numbers one to nine down solid. Tell your child that you need his help to create a number game.

What to Do

Making the Game

1 Cut the cardboard into cards of the following sizes and numbers:

nine cards, 4 inches by 1 inch (10 by 2 cm)

nine cards, 3 inches by 1 inch (8 by 2 cm)

nine cards, 2 inches by 1 inch (5 by 2 cm)

nine cards, 1 inch by 1 inch (2 by 2 cm)

2 Using the ruler and pencil, divide each card into squares of about 1 inch (2 cm).

3 Use the marking pen to write numerals on the cards as follows, keeping one numeral in each 1-inch (2-cm) space:

On the biggest cards, write the even thousands, 1000 to 9000

On the next biggest cards, write the even hundreds, 100 to 900

On the third biggest cards, write the even tens, 10 to 90

On the smallest cards, write 1 to 9

Using the Cards (Read through all the remaining steps before trying this with your child.)

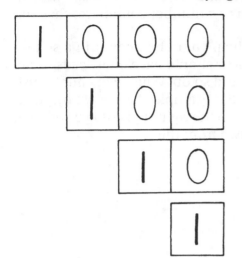

4   Start with the 1 card. Place it on a table and ask your child to count out loud with you.

5   Tell your child that this is how each numeral looks written down. Go through the cards 1 to 9. Ask your child to show you each number on his fingers or with counters. *Always use the counters as you work with these cards until your child begins on his own to work without them.*

6   Say to your child, "I wonder what'll happen when we get to 10."

7   Put the 10 card down in front of your child. Ask, "How come this zero is here?" (One possible explanation is that all the fingers have been counted through once and no more.)

8   Show your child that adding another finger or counter after 9 requires adding another numeral in the ones column. Stack the 1 card on top of the zero on the 10 card. Go on up through the teens until you reach 20. Once again, ask your child why the zero is there, and what the 2 stands for.

Follow-up Activities

• Depending on your child's level of understanding and interest, continue up to 100 and eventually to 1000.

• Make cards showing a numeral for your child to replicate. For example, make a card the same size as the thousands card, and write 1,372 on it. Your child will make this numeral with the 1000 card, the 300 card, the 70 card, and the 2 card.

What's Happening

As your child counts, using higher and higher numbers, he needs a system for keeping track of what he counts. Our number system seems quirky, however, until it's broken down and understood bit by bit. The best way to do this is through concrete experience—counting and manipulating objects—and through number cards that are themselves manipulable and countable. As your child works with these cards over and over, he'll begin to comprehend the patterns by which places are filled "to the nines" and replaced with zeros (which are really the tail end of tens).

Moving Ahead   Have your child set up a number with the cards. Then ask him to add 2, and then 2 more, and so on. Encourage him to explain what happens when one number column reaches 10.

Helpful Hint   Use or make an abacus to help your child count in a similar manner. Each rod of the abacus should have nine beads. Label the rods "1s," "10s," "100s," and so on. When you count, push the beads from left to right. For example, 3 is shown by pushing three beads on the 1s rod to the right; 12 is shown with one bead from the 10s rod and two from the 1s.

11 'Rithmetic Rods

Helps develop: *conservation of number, one-to-one correspondence, addition and subtraction, symbolic representation of arithmetic functions*

You can buy toys like these, but they are much more valuable and understandable to your child when she makes them herself with you at her side.

You'll Need   a 60-inch (150-cm) piece of 1-by-1-inch (2.5-by-2.5-cm) wood; ruler; pencil; saw; sandpaper; paint in two colors; brushes

Before You Begin   Read through these directions with your child. Track down the materials and set them up in a work area.

What to Do   **Making the Game**

1 Use the pencil and ruler to divide the entire length of the wood into 1-inch (2.5-cm) segments.

2 Use a heavier line of pencil to mark the wood for cutting as follows. You'll need a 1-inch (2.5-cm) piece, a 2-inch (5-cm) piece, a 3-inch (7.5-cm) piece, and so on up to a 10-inch (25-cm) piece.

3 Cut the wood with the saw. There will be one 5-inch (12.5-cm) piece left over. Discard it.

4 Work with your child to sand the wood.

5 Over the course of two days, paint your lengths of wood. The 1-inch (2.5-cm) piece and the first 1-inch (2.5-cm) segment of every length should be the same color: for example, red. The second segment of each piece should be another color: for example, blue. The third segment will be red again, the fourth blue, and so on, until all the even numbers are one color and all the odd numbers are the other color.

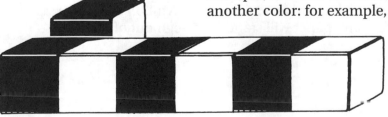

Playing the Game

6 Let your child explore the pieces of the new game.

7 Pick up a piece. Name it with the number of segments it has, without counting the segments. That is, say "This is the 3," not "This is the 1-2-3." Say, "I wonder what is the same as the 3?" Compare, with your child, the 3 to the other lengths. Introduce the idea that two smaller lengths (1 and 2), together, are the same as the 3.

Follow-up Activity

Invite your child to choose one number rod. Ask, "I wonder what is the same?" Have your child place the number rod horizontally in front of her and then line up other rods beneath it to see which combinations come out to the same length.

What's Happening

When she's had plenty of experience with this game, your child will be able to compare lengths of objects and will understand that the number 7 is divisible into 7 equal parts—into 2 and 5, into 3 and 4, and into 6 and 1. As she proceeds to symbolic representations of these basic arithmetic concepts, she'll have the rods to support her, first as hands-on manipulatives to prove her calculations, then as objects to envision as she works calculations in her head.

Moving Ahead

Lay a rod at the top of a standard letter-size sheet of paper placed sideways. Have your child figure out, as above, which smaller rods work together to equal the larger one. Help your child to record her work by writing the numerals in the space beside each rod. For example, the top row says *8*. The next row says *7* and *1*. Show your child the symbols + and = and explain their purpose. Guide your child to represent her arrangement of the rods by writing *7 + 1 = 8*.

Helpful Hint

Have your child use graph paper with large squares to draw her rods and record her calculations symbolically. Each square on the graph paper will stand for a segment of a rod.

12 Bead Stair

Double- and triple-digit numbers can be confusing. This will help your child understand that 42 really means four tens and two ones.

You'll Need   pipe cleaners; beads

Before You Begin   Start this activity when your child is comfortable counting to 10 and higher.

What to Do

1 Say, "This is starting to be too many to count them every time." Suggest stringing ten beads onto a pipe cleaner. Have your child count the beads as he strings them. "Okay, that's ten." Make a crimp or knot in the end of the pipe cleaner.

2 Make another pipe cleaner of beads. How many all together: the first ten, then one more, two more, and so on?

3 Continue making bead stairs (I call them this because the beads move up the pipe cleaners in steps, as does the child's counting: "Two tens seven units; two tens eight units; two tens nine units; three tens") until you reach one hundred. Then ask your child, "How can we hook them together to show there are one hundred of them?"

Follow-up Activity   Make as many bead stairs as you want. Keep loose beads on hand, too. Use them as counters to show various numbers.

Moving Ahead   Invite your child to draw pictures of bead stairs and number each bead.

Helpful Hint   This activity demonstrates base ten. To introduce other base systems to your child, change the limit on beads for each bead stair. For example, for the binary (base two) system, there would be only one bead in the ones. Two beads would be a ten.

13 Pyramid of Tens

*Solitaire is a good occupation for your child, allowing her
to take her own time, challenge her own patience level,
and learn about math operations, while moving
as slowly or quickly as her ability dictates.*

You'll Need   a deck of playing cards

Before You Begin   Teach this game to a child who has had ample experience
working with numerals and numbers up to ten. This is a good
game for a child who is working on basic arithmetic in school.

What to Do   **1** Lay out your cards face up in a pyramid shape as follows:
one card at the top, two cards overlapping that card, three
cards overlapping the two row, and so on, until there are
seven cards at the bottom of the pyramid.

2 The point of the game is to find a
pair of numbers that add up to ten
and to discard them. Only cards
with no other cards overlapping
them may be used. The King,
Queen, and Jack equal ten, and
they and the 10 can be discarded as soon as they are
uncovered. The combina-
tions are as follows:

9 + ace (1) = 10

8 + 2 = 10

7 + 3 = 10

6 + 4 = 10

5 + 5 = 10

3 Begin by seeing if any cards not covered by other cards can be combined to make ten. Discard them. Do this until there are no combinations to be made.

4 Go through the cards left over from dealing (not the discards) to match up with the pyramid cards that remain. But you can still match and discard only the uncovered cards.

5 If you can discard all the cards in the pyramid, you win.

Follow-up Activities

• Talk about whether this game would work with a total other than ten. Why or why not?

• Try laying out the cards in piles that add up to ten. How many ways are there to arrange the cards?

What's Happening

A child who plays this game quickly becomes conversant with all the numbers that combine to make ten. She also must use strategy to determine which cards to combine and to determine whether she has a good pyramid or one that has no possible moves. She also learns something about probability, the luck of the draw that determines the configuration of cards in the pyramid, for better or worse.

Moving Ahead

Play Go Fish (Activity 53) with a variation. Instead of fishing for matching denominations, fish for cards that work with the cards in your hand to add up to ten. Any face card is discarded (or could be left out of the deal). A player who has an 8 in his hand fishes for a 2 to match up with it. Play ends when one player runs out of cards.

Helpful Hint

Remind your child to use the pictures of suit symbols on the cards to find combinations that add up to ten. For example, the three of diamonds has three diamonds on it. The seven of clubs has seven clubs. Your child can count these up to find the total of ten.

14 Add In, Take Out

- -

Helps develop: *understanding of addition and subtraction and the reversibility of arithmetic, one-to-one correspondence, probability*

This game takes computation symbols (+ and –) and numerals and makes them real to your child.

- -

You'll Need muffin tins or artists' palettes with indentations (these are your game boards; you need one per player); a spinner from a board game, relabeled so that the spinner points to numerals 1 to 5; a die, relabeled so that three sides show + (plus) symbols and three sides show – (minus) symbols; counters: small beans or bingo chips

Before You Begin Play this game with a child who has had plenty of experience counting numbers up to ten.

What to Do
1 The first player spins.
2 The player reads the numeral on the spinner and counts that many counters into his board, one per cup or indentation.
3 The next player spins and counts out the appropriate number also.
4 The first player goes again. This time he rolls the die first to see if he must add or take away. Then he spins the spinner to determine how many to add or take away. If he adds, he counts the given number into the cups as before. If he subtracts, he takes counters out of the cups. *There are no negative numbers. Subtract only to zero.* Then the player must give the total for his turn.
5 Play continues as in step 4, as each player rolls the die to see what must be done and spins the spinner to find the number it must be done with.

Follow-up Activity   Encourage your child to experiment with different kinds of counters and eventually, tallies: ||||| |||

What's Happening   *Through playing this game, your child sees that one pile of counters can be grouped and regrouped, removed from and added to in many different ways to come up with different numbers. This is the stuff math is made of: the patterns of the numbers and numerals, the relationships between them, the way they look and feel and change.*

Moving Ahead   Keep track of each turn by writing the operation in number-sentence form: $1 + 4 = 5$, for example.

Helpful Hint   Instead of a spinner, use a box of number cards, an octahedron die (a die with eight sides), or two dice.

15 Take a Vote

Take a Vote

Helps develop: *sorting, graphing information, understanding sets*

Help your child take a survey and graph the results. It's a method of understanding people and data that will take her through college.

You'll Need   paper; solid-colored stickers; pen

Before You Begin   Look for an opportunity to use this activity to follow up on some family discussion: what to have for dinner, where to go for a walk, who likes broccoli and who doesn't.

What to Do
1 When the discussion point has been raised, grab the materials above and say something like, "We seem to have a difference of opinion. I would like to see how this looks on paper. Everybody, hold your vote."

2 Draw vertical lines on the paper to make as many columns as necessary to have a column for each kind of answer.

3 Have your child ask each person to give an opinion about the topic at hand. That is, ask one family member whether or not she likes broccoli. Suppose she says yes. Ask your child, "How should we label this?"—*Likes Broccoli* or something to that effect. Write this at the top of the column. Have the person write her name on a sticker and place it at the bottom of the column.

4 Place successive stickers above one another in a vertical line.

5 Continue polling your group until everyone has placed a sticker on the graph.

6 Talk about what the results show. You might ask your child, "What does this graph tell you about this group?"

Follow-up Activity   Take votes about other topics of your child's choosing. Graph them.

Moving Ahead Use the same materials and information to create a Venn diagram of these data, as shown in the illustration.

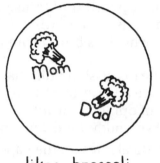 

likes broccoli   doesn't like broccoli

Helpful Hint A younger child can get a firm grip on the graphing idea by gathering toothbrushes from each person in the household and grouping them according to colors. Make a large graph that shows the colors of toothbrushes in your house, then place each toothbrush in the appropriate column. This provides a more physical representation than the stickers do. For another simple graph, see Activity 2: Family Pictures.

PART TWO

Space, Shape, and Measurement

Your child has been exploring space since she first moved from one side of her crib to the other. She's still doing it, every time she draws, walks, builds, climbs, looks around a room, or studies the horizon. Now she needs to use and increase that understanding of space to solve new problems, to share her designs, to record what she observes.

This section provides a wealth of interesting ingredients to add to the math stew you're creating in your home. Take every opportunity to experiment, explore, measure, discuss, and enjoy.

16 Tall Book, Small Book

Helps develop:
*making compar-
isons according to
attributes*

*What's the tallest thing your child knows?
What's the smallest thing he knows?*

You'll Need   construction paper; stapler *or* needle and thread; crayons or markers

Before You Begin   Help your child see that *tall* and *short* are relative terms. What's tall to a child might not be tall to an adult; what's tall to a spider might not be tall to a cat.

What to Do

1 Have your child help you cut construction paper lengthwise and form it into a tall book. Staple one end or fasten it with needle and thread.

2 Cut small squares of paper and form them into a small book in the same manner.

3 Ask your child to fill the tall book with pictures of tall things, and the small book with pictures of small things. He can draw the pictures with crayons or markers.

4 Talk about the pictures in the books. To whom does a giraffe appear tall? To whom does a mushroom appear tall? What in this book is taller than a skyscraper? What's smaller than a mouse?

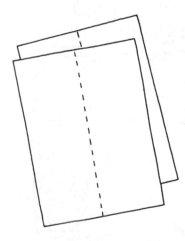

MY
TALL
BOOK

Follow-up Activity

Have your child make one book showing tall and short things side by side. Note that this is more complicated because of the need to show relative size.

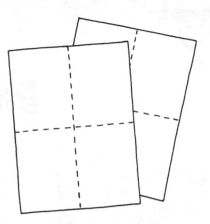

What's Happening

Making these books gives your child an opportunity to explore a full range of sizes and learn the language that is used to compare and describe them.

Moving Ahead   Make wide books, narrow books, and long books.

Helpful Hint   Talk about relative sizes of "families" of objects in your child's toy collection; for example, matryoshkas (Russian nesting dolls) or other toys that fit inside each other, animal families, and travel-sized games.

17 Pick It Up,
Pack It Up

*elps develop:
understanding
of space, use of area
and perimeter,
relationship between
shapes and spaces*

*The old circus gag of dozens of clowns climbing out of
a tiny car makes your child laugh because she knows
so many clowns couldn't possibly fit in there—or could they?*

You'll Need a plastic carrying case or small suitcase; dress-up clothes, foam
blocks, or whatever items you'd like your child to store in the
case

Before You Begin Establish that this case is for storing and carrying the items in
question. Help your child understand the need for storing
these in one particular place: to keep the pieces together, to
help them fit in the toy closet, and so on. Be sure the items
really will fit into the case. (Try it yourself first.)

What to Do 1 Lay the items out beside the suitcase, spreading out all the
pieces. Ask your child, "Do you think we'll be able to fit all
this stuff into the case?"

2 Encourage your child to experiment with different configu-
rations. Do the foam blocks need to be fit together? Can the
clothes be consolidated in any way? Which works better
with clothes—rolling, folding, or just stuffing them in?

3 If the items don't fit one way, encourage your child to
dump them all out and try again another way.

4 Got it all in? Great! Recap how it was done to help you both
remember how to do it next time.

Follow-up Activities • Find containers for as many toys as possible, and let your
child figure out the best way to pack them up. Then fit the
containers into the toy storage area.

- Organize (with your child's help) your child's drawers, the medicine cabinet, the junk drawer, and so on, in a similar manner. Ask her advice all the way. "Where should we put this?" "Can you move this over so there's more room?"

What's Happening

*S*pace is something each of us must deal with on a daily basis. Organizing not only helps your child keep track of things, but gives her valuable experience in using shapes within spaces in different ways, arranging them and rearranging them to find the way they fit best. As your child arranges toys, she learns about the properties of different shapes and how they relate to one another. Soft cloth can be mushed, crushed, and rolled, to eliminate air. Squares can be fitted together side by side to use space most efficiently. You can get this point across to your child in many ways: by talking with her about the storage potential of your refrigerator when you use square containers instead of round ones, by encouraging her to become involved in packing the car for a trip, and by letting her draw her own conclusions about that circus trick.

Moving Ahead

Encourage your child to use tangrams, a commonly available game. Usually a tangrams set comes with a pack of cards showing the outline of shapes: animals, buildings, and geometric shapes. The seven tangrams (small geometric shapes) must be fitted into each outline. Mastering tangrams requires learning to see, manipulate, rotate, and understand each shape in a new way in relation to the others for every single outline.

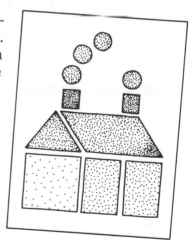

Helpful Hint

Have your child make her own jigsaw puzzles by gluing drawings to thin cardboard and cutting them into smaller pieces. She'll gain an understanding of how shapes fit together to make a larger picture, and she'll easily master fitting her own artwork together.

18 Sock Scale

*Each sock holds a mystery object.
Let your child close his eyes and feel.*

Helps develop:
*concept of weight,
making comparisons,
making nonstandard
measurements*

You'll Need   two old socks; a variety of objects

Before You Begin   Discuss with your child: What makes something heavy? What does it mean to be heavy? How do you decide whether something is heavy or light?

What to Do
1 Have your child close his eyes.

2 Place an object in each sock. Use objects with obviously different weights: a baseball and an eraser, a pencil and a rock, and so on. Let the objects fall into the sock's toe.

3 Have your child hold the top of both socks, one in each hand.

4 Ask, "Which is heavier? Which is lighter?"

Follow-up Activities
• Work up to using objects that are close in weight. Listen to the words your child uses to describe the differences between them: heavier, heaviest, a little heavier, a little lighter, and so on.

• Have your child load objects into the socks while you decide which is heavier.

• Use a scale to measure and compare the weight of the objects.

• Have your child hold the objects in the palms of his hands instead of in the sock.

What's Happening

When you have your child weigh things without looking, you encourage him to focus on his basic sense of touch and refine his ability to compare. When you place the objects in the socks instead of in his hands and have him close his eyes, he assesses weight, rather than size, texture, or anything else that might be observed about an object. Language helps him to make the experience more abstract.

Your child will more easily understand standard measurements such as grams and pounds if he has already explored nonstandard measurements. These may be rocks, potatoes, or objects that are of a uniform weight, such as baseballs or coffee cans. Once your child understands that one object may weigh the same as two baseballs, while another object weighs three baseballs, he's ready to hear about ways that other people have devised to weigh things— using standards so that everyone understands.

Moving Ahead

Ask your child to choose two objects from the assortment and predict which will be heaviest. Then compare them, using the sock scale.

Helpful Hint

Use the sock scale with Activity 24: Can You Weight? to balance objects with nonstandard weights.

19 Making Models

There was something missing from the model of the new school building. The kids went to the art cart, made people of twist-ties from bread bags, cotton balls, and colored paper, and added them to the model. Not even built yet, the school was already theirs.

Helps develop: *understanding the concept of scale (relative size), analysis of pattern and design*

You'll Need

a variety of odds and ends including such items as cardboard, yarn, wood, glue, straws, straw, wheels, foil, paper, etc.

Before You Begin

Do this activity as an outgrowth of your child's interest in something in the world: a building, a vehicle, a living creature. The idea is to create a model that can fit on a sheet of cardboard, whether the original item is minuscule (a cricket) or huge (a front-loading tractor). Use a workbench or outdoor table for your construction, as this will be messy.

What to Do

1 Suggest making a model of an object that interests your child. Show her the assortment of materials you've assembled. Ask her how they can be used to create the model. What parts need to be included? What sorts of shapes and sizes are involved?

2 Help with mechanics: nailing, screwing, gluing, drying, painting, and measuring. Let your child determine what goes where and what is needed.

3 Encourage your child to pose problems such as, "How can I make table legs?" Encourage her to solve problems with materials you have on hand unless there's something needed that absolutely must be purchased.

4 Compare the model side by side with the real-life item. How are they different? How are they the same?

Follow-up Activities

• If your child has made a miniature, suggest that she consider what would be required to make a large version. It's fun to imagine, "How large would a giant's version of a skyscraper (or a toothbrush, or a car) be?"

- If your child has made a large-scale version, consider asking her to make a miniature of something else. The idea that you can make an elephant the same size as a cricket is intriguing—and opens the door to wonderful stories.

What's Happening   *When your child draws a person on paper and says that it's Mommy, she's actually drawing a familiar object in miniature. Kids see a lot of miniatures: a great portion of your child's toys are probably small versions of real-life things (trains, cars, planes, dolls, kids' stoves, workbenches, tools, and so on). Miniatures bring large objects down to a manageable level for your child. But it's useful to make small things larger to get a clearer picture of their form and function. Get your child making her own models and you help her get a handle on the proportions of the world.*

Moving Ahead   Copy machines with reduction and enlargement functions are fascinating to children as well as adults. Take a favorite book to a copy machine—or just use your child's hands. Show your child how to operate the machine to create large and small versions of the subject, and even reduce the reductions further or enlarge the enlargements until only a portion of the original subject comes out. Take the copies home and hang them on a wall or lay them on the floor. How do they compare to the original?

Helpful Hint   Origami (Japanese paper folding) is a way of creating models out of paper. Origami models are generally somewhat abstract. Sometimes they're miniatures, sometimes they're enlargements. See Activity 29: Hats On! or a book on origami.

20 Giant Steps

"Mother, may I?"
This classic game is not only fun, it helps your child
become adept at estimating distances and space.

Helps develop:
understanding of
measurement, area,
and perimeter, gross
motor movement

You'll Need   a space wide enough for all your players to move around

Before You Begin   This game can be played almost anytime, almost anywhere, with any number of players of pretty much any age. Let everyone get a chance to be "Mother."

What to Do   1 Assign one player to be "Mother." Mother, the leader of the game, stands at one side of the playing space, the finish line. The players stand in a row at the other side of the space, the starting line.

2 Mother chooses a player to be first and gives that player an assignment. For example, "Jason, you may take three giant steps."

Here are examples of other kinds of steps that may be assigned:

giant steps—as far as the leg can reach

baby steps—tiny steps close together. About ten baby steps equal one giant step

kangaroo hops—big jumps with the feet together

frog hops—similar to kangaroo hops, but smaller

umbrella twirls—movements in a forward direction while twirling, with an arm overhead as though carrying an umbrella

tiptoes—small steps on tiptoe

duck walks—waddling steps moving slowly forward

You can also assign skips, hops, running leaps and so on, or you can make up your own steps or order that steps be done backward toward the starting line.

3 Before moving, the player must ask, "Mother, may I?" If he forgets to say this, he returns to the starting line.

4 Mother may answer, "Yes, you may," or "No, you may not." If Mother says no, the player must stay where he is.

5 Play continues until all players have reached the finish line. The last person to get to the finish line is Mother next time.

Follow-up Activity Talk about distances in terms of different kinds of steps: "How many baby steps would it take to get from the bedroom to the bathroom? How many kangaroo hops?" Encourage your child to estimate, then test his theory.

What's Happening *Children who play this game very quickly figure out that they can reach the finish line more quickly with giant steps than with baby steps. The entire game involves nonstandard measurement—the crossing of an area through movements that are regulated only by the size of the person performing them. Children also figure out equations; they know they'd rather do three umbrella steps than three giant steps, because umbrella steps can be stretched out. They have a shape that can be expanded. Kangaroo hops and frog hops, too, are variable depending on whether more energy is put into moving forward or up in the air.*

Moving Ahead Suggest that players make deals with Mother. When Mother gives them an order, they may say something like, "Mother dear, may I take two frog hops and an umbrella step instead?" Mother must determine whether what they're asking for is equal to her order before deciding whether to say "Yes, you may," or "No, you may not."

Helpful Hint Watch animals move on television with your child: there's that beautiful elephant swimming on the soft-drink commercial, penguins tottering along, cats cha-cha-ing, etc. Use what you discover to create some new steps for this game. Talk about how the animals' forms dictate their movements.

21 Box Buildings

Helps develop: understanding of weight, height, perimeter and area, three-dimensional thinking and planning skills

Round buildings, square houses, teepees, skyscrapers, cliff dwellings, igloos—the possibilities of building buildings are endless!

You'll Need many cardboard boxes of various shapes and sizes; masking tape; scissors, fabric, flag, crayons, markers (optional)

Before You Begin Bring in a pile of boxes. Ask your child to think about what she could build with the boxes.

What to Do

1 Talk with your child about what she'd like to build. Ask her to decide with you where to build her structure.

2 Use masking tape to outline a space on the floor for the building to fill. Make it clear that this is not a line over which your child's construction must not stray; it's mainly a guideline for the basic perimeter of the structure.

3 Help your child build, or (if she wishes) have her build on her own or with another child. Discuss what's going on as she works, asking her to talk about what she's thinking and planning. "How high would you like it to be?" "I wonder what you'll think of for the roof . . ."

4 Invite your child to decorate her building with extra materials you have on hand.

Follow-up Activity Encourage your child to find ways to make windows, doors, and furniture.

In order to be able to eventually work symbolically, children need to have real experiences. Children who will be expected to understand area, perimeter, three-dimensional models, and two-dimensional diagrams should be encouraged to build forts, houses, boats, trains, dollhouses, and all sorts of other block constructions. This activity teaches children—through experience and exploration—how objects occupy space.

Moving Ahead Encourage your child to plan or reconstruct a building by creating a small block model of it, using blocks of similar shape and proportion to the boxes.

Helpful Hint Liquor-store boxes are especially strong and will hold up well to repeated building. Appliance boxes, while shorter lived, provide valuable experience dealing with larger materials and space.

22 (No Use Crying Over) Spilt Milk!

Helps develop: *flexibility in thinking, visual identification, replication of patterns*

An eminent mathematician grew up with a mother who reacted calmly when he spilled his milk. They drew shapes in the liquid. Here's how you can put your child's curiosity—and every opportunity born of natural causes—to use.

You'll Need newspaper or newsprint; containers from which liquid can be poured, spilled, dropped: eyedropper, drinking straws, plastic cups, watering can; permanent marker; water with food coloring in it *or* milk

Before You Begin Okay, you know it's going to happen: your child's milk will eventually tip over. Rein in your natural response and leave the milk on the table. Observe how it soaks into the tablecloth. Trace its path onto the floor. Then, and only then, assess how many sponges it takes to mop it up.

What to Do

1 Add to (or make up for your inability to stomach) the Before You Begin activity by creating spillage with your child. Go outside with your equipment. Lay a sheet of newspaper on the ground and label it with the name or a drawing of the container your child is going to pour from.

2 Ask your child to fill the container with water and spill it onto the newspaper. Together, watch the water spread and soak into the paper. You may want to moderate the amount of water dumped.

3 Have your child use the marker to draw a boundary around the spill showing its shape and how far it spread.

4 Pour water on several more sheets, using containers of different sizes, and again have your child mark the edges of the spills.

5 Hang the sheets, or lay them flat to dry. Ask your child to check them from time to time, noting which dries most quickly, which most slowly.

6 Examine the results. Wonder, with your child, how water could take so many different shapes.

Follow-up Activities
- Try different liquids. Do they all behave the same as water?
- Use an eyedropper and small pieces of material, paper, plastic.

What's Happening   This activity drives home the point that patterns occur naturally and spontaneously in nature. Through repeated experimentation, your child realizes that an action he takes has a similar—but infinitely varied—pattern for a result.

Moving Ahead   Provide a sketchbook and suggest that your child examine, sketch, and discuss other natural patterns: the ripples in water when a rock falls in, a spider's web, a sunset, the way branches splay out from the trunks of trees. Discuss man-made patterns, too. Ask your child to search the house for good examples such as the spiral of a notebook, the fabric of sheets, the ribbed edge of a glue bottle, the fluted edge of a paper plate, and so on.

Helpful Hint   *It Looked Like Spilt Milk* by Fulvio Testa is a picture book in which an artist finds shapes in milk drops just as many of us do in clouds.

23 Print 'n' Press

Helps develop: *knowledge of the properties of geometric figures, understanding that patterns are reversible*

A surprising number of adults, asked to draw an island showing how it looks underwater, draw a blob that appears to be floating. They probably never thought about the fact that an island is a hill partly covered with water. This activity allows your child to explore the flat planes of a three-dimensional object.

You'll Need

blocks: cylinders, square cylinders, pyramids, squares, rectangles, and other blocks; pencils with erasers; other printing equipment: rubber stamps, carrots, potatoes, apples, and so on; washable water-base paint; drawing paper

Before You Begin

Using washable paint, have your child paint her hand and make a print of it (more effective and interesting for the child than just placing her hand in paint). Talk about the image that appears. In what way does it resemble the hand? In what ways is it dissimilar?

What to Do

1 Get out some blocks. Ask your child what she thinks would happen if these blocks were used for printing. What would the image from this side be? From this end?

2 Lay out some paper and let your child go to town, painting and then printing the blocks in as many angles and colors as she wants.

3 When she's done several, talk about the various shapes and match them up with the blocks that created them. Why, ask your child, does a cylinder make a circle? Why does a pyramid (a four-sided one) make a square?

Follow-up Activities

- Which shapes make big impressions? Which shapes make smaller ones? Suggest that your child print a series based on size.

- Make available an assortment of printing goods. Go on a hunt for more household materials that would be interesting to print. Try buttons, pennies, hairpins, and so on. Invite your child to add to her design or to create a new one using these materials.

- Make refrigerator cookies, the kind that require rolling dough into a log and cutting slices. Let your child experiment with forming the log into different shapes, then slicing.

What's Happening

A prism—such as a cylinder or a pyramid—is a three-dimensional geometric shape formed from parallel planes. This activity shows the planes that make up a three-dimensional object. Whatever a stamp's shape, it only prints the bottom, outermost plane. This is especially pertinent information when it comes to prisms. You can see that a cylinder is what would result if you could weld a stack of circles together. And what you get when you print a cylinder is a circle. Strange, isn't it, that a pyramid is really made up of squares, one atop another, until the top one is merely a point?

Moving Ahead

Invite your child to cut her own stamps from carrots or potatoes, or from wood or linoleum blocks. Explore, also, the textures and shapes of these items, to see the different prints that can be formed. What do you get, for example, when you cut an apple in half lengthwise and print the half? What happens when you cut it in half horizontally?

Helpful Hint

Your child's design can be made into a rubber stamp by many print shops. Your child will be fascinated by the process, which involves copying the design, reversing it, recreating it from rubber, and gluing it onto a stamp. Then, when it's inked and stamped, the design is frontward again! Awesome!

24 Can You Weight?

Your child will understand the concept of measuring weight better if he learns by comparing weights of objects he knows before using the scale.

You'll Need

modeling clay or dough; containers; objects for weighing; a balance scale with two trays *or* a seesaw with the fulcrum at the center

Before You Begin

Try Activity 18: Sock Scale before this one. Allow your child to explore a balance scale or seesaw to determine how to make it balance with hand pressure or by laying objects on either side.

What to Do

1 Wait until your child has succeeded in balancing something precisely on the scale or seesaw. Discuss it. "So, a baseball glove weighs the same as two potatoes? That's interesting."

2 Say, "Hey, I wonder which weighs more? The baseball glove or the football?"

3 Create your own weights. Make a ball of clay or dough, or pick up something else small that you have a lot of. It should be something that has a fairly uniform size, such as dough balls, pencils, or pennies. Have your child choose something to use as his own measurement standard, and name it for him. Choose your own standard, and name it for yourself.

4 Now weigh each thing, using your standard. Put the object to be weighed on one side of the scale, and slowly add weights to the other side until the scale balances.

5 Record what each item weighs, in your own standards.

Item	Weight in Marlenes	Weight in Karens
baseball glove	2 Marlenes	4 Karens
baseball	3 Marlenes	6 Karens

6 Talk about your discoveries with your child. What makes one thing heavier than another?

Follow-up Activity Sooner or later, your child may say, "Wouldn't it be easier to have just one way to measure?" This is when you say, "As a matter of fact, someone has already thought of that." Introduce the idea of ounces and pounds, or grams and kilograms. Use a standard scale to compare the weight in ounces or grams to your nonstandard measurements.

What's Happening *This activity lets your child see what weight measurements really mean. It might seem simpler and more direct to just start off with ounces and grams, but they won't mean as much before your child has experimented with creating his own system of weight measurement. They're just numbers, and carry no weight of their own. Scales that use counter-weights—weights of known amounts that balance against the item being weighed—are the most graphic illustration of the process of measuring weight. Children who use only digital scales or the spring scales in grocery stores never really understand the process. Rather, the arrow points, like magic, or those digital numbers appear, with an even more magical spoken message. This activity lets your child get his hands on the message behind the magic.*

Moving Ahead If you didn't use a seesaw for your weight comparisons, make one now from a few bricks and a board. Move the fulcrum, and experiment with using weight and leverage to move an object on the other end. Talk to your child about what balancing means to weight.

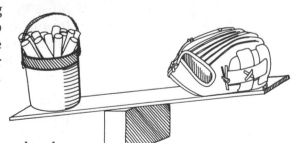

Helpful Hint In the grocery store or hardware shop, talk with your child about the different measurements used to weigh solids and liquids. Have him compare the weights of quarts of juice to the weights of half-gallons of juice.

25 How You Measure Up

Helps develop: *flexibility in thinking, problem solving, understanding of standards and principles of measurement*

As with measuring weight, your child will understand the concept of measuring length if she uses something she knows to measure—her thumb, her foot, or a crayon.

You'll Need   poster board; markers; yardstick (meterstick) *or* tape measure

Before You Begin   Get this one started by asking your child to help you measure a distance.

What to Do

1 Suggest finding a way to measure a short distance or the length of a common object. Ask questions such as "I wonder how many of my feet it is from one side of the room to the other?" or "I wonder how many hands long this table is?"

2 Talk with your child about common standards of measurement, such as feet, hands (to measure the height of horses), and inches.

3 Measure the distance in question using your own feet or thumb, and also your child's feet or thumb. Use the poster board to make a chart comparing several distances or lengths. Name the standards of measurement with your child; for example, "Bonnie's Feet."

4 What else could be used to measure? Use model cars, ballpoint pens, crayons, or whatever your child suggests as a standard of measurement. Add a few new standards of measurement to the chart.

Follow-up Activities

• Talk about whether people really need to use standards of measurement. Why or why not?

- Make your own measuring stick by painting one side of an old yardstick or meterstick and marking it according to one of your new standards of measurement. If you're using crayons, for example, lay one crayon along the yardstick, with its end at the end of the stick. Draw a mark on the yardstick at the other end of the crayon and label it *1*. Continue down the yardstick, marking crayon lengths.

What's Happening

A yardstick, a meterstick, and a measuring tape are really all a series of inches or centimeters side by side. Your child is more likely to recognize that something measures longer or shorter than the stick than she is to understand that the object measures a number of inches or centimeters long—that is, until you take the system apart. By the end of this activity your child sees measurement as a flexible tool, created for people, by people, for the purpose of communicating a mathematical concept.

Moving Ahead   Invite your child to experiment with square measures by cutting 1-inch (2-cm) squares from white paper. Have your child explore putting the squares down in various formations to make islands: how many islands can you make that measure 6 square inches (12 cm^2)?

Helpful Hint   Gather a box of ribbons and strings of different lengths. Encourage your child to arrange them, with much discussion of comparative length. "These are almost the same." Measure to see if there is a slight difference. Talk about which is the longest, shortest, widest, and so on.

26 Just Trying to Fit In

Helps develop: *understanding of capacity, volume, area, measurement, and properties of shapes*

Children know from observation that rectangles and squares fit together into patterns that can go wall to wall, curb to curb, floor to ceiling. But what shapes fit best in a box? In a jar? In a flat template?

You'll Need
a variety of containers; sand; a variety of small objects: marbles, tiles, pennies, etc.; measuring cup or large jar; marking pen that writes on glass; paper and pencil (optional)

Before You Begin
This activity can be done with any kind of container and any kind of filling material. The key is to make comparisons between containers or between materials, or between both.

What to Do

1 Present your child with two or three containers to choose from. Ask, "I wonder which of these can hold the most sand?"

2 Invite your child to figure out which container has the greatest capacity for holding sand. One way to do this is to have him fill the container with as much as possible and then dump the sand from that container into an even larger jar and mark the sand line on the larger jar with a pen. He can then dump the sand out, leaving the mark there for comparison with later loads, and move on to the next container. Or he can see how many of one container it takes to fill the larger jar.

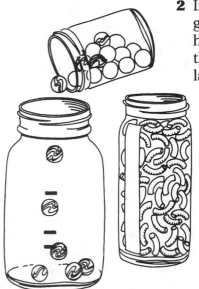

3 Talk about the results with your child. Also discuss the best way to transfer sand from the sandbox or bag of sand to the container. What is the most efficient: Spoon? Cup? Box?

4 Ask your child to choose one tool for transferring sand, such as a cup. Help him make a graph with a column of cups for each container, showing how many cups it took to fill each one.

Follow-up Activities
- Have your child help you select boxes for storage or gift giving, noting the kind of object or size of object it might hold.
- Use an artist's template or any cutout shape. Ask your child to fit as many pennies as possible into this shape. Which shape holds the most pennies? Next try Scrabble tiles or something else small and square. How many of these fit into the shape?
- Have your child fill a large container (the sink, a washtub) using a spoon, a cup, an eyedropper, a baby bottle. How many does he think it will take? How many *does* it take?

What's Happening Your child is exploring *different ways in which objects of varying shape take up space. Sand is great because it molds itself to the actual capacity of the container. Marbles do not. These things are learned through experimenting. The more experiments, the better for your child.*

Moving Ahead Once your child has determined how much sand fits into a container, have him compare the weight of dry and wet sand in the same container.

Helpful Hint Make corn bread or brownies in pans of different shapes on successive occasions. Have your child cut them up into squares or triangles for eating. Help him note that round pans make cakes that slice best into triangular wedges, while square cakes can be cut into block pieces. Cut out a slice, lift it from the pan, then show how it fits back in. The piece of cake occupies its own space!

27 On the Road to Somewhere

On the Road to Somewhere

Helps develop: *physical confidence with area, understanding of spatial relationships and lines, one-to-one correspondence*

Show your child how to make Chutes and Ladders life-size in your backyard or living room!

You'll Need   construction paper; masking tape; miscellaneous stuffed animals, toys, blocks

Before You Begin   Choose a board game that involves following a path to get to a goal: Chutes and Ladders, Candyland, Sorry, or any other favorite. Familiarize your child with the rules of the board game.

What to Do   **1** Tell your child that you're going to make a giant version of your game. Ask your child to help you make a list of pieces you'll need and to give you ideas for making the game board.

2 Use one sheet of construction paper for each landing spot on your board. You'll probably want to use fewer landing spots than in the actual game. Use colors that match the ones on the board, or mark the spots with words and symbols that match the board. Tape the spots to the floor. (It's best to play barefoot or in stocking feet to cut down on wear and tear to your game.)

3 Use construction paper to create cards and other things that you'll need to play the game. You can use the spinner or dice from the board game. You won't need players' tokens, because you and your child will be the tokens, moving from space to space.

4 If there are intermediate goals along the path of the game board, such as Plumpy and Lord Licorice in Candyland, create these using stuffed animals, signs or pictures, or building blocks. Make a goal for the end of the game in a similar manner.

5 Play the game. Follow the board game rules for the most part. Encourage your child to count the number of spaces she's allowed to move by saying the numeral as she walks.

Follow-up Activity

Extend this basic concept to other board games. The more you play with this idea, the more your child will develop ease and creativity in working in different scales.

What's Happening

One of the first things that you learn when you play a board game is to follow the path of play. One of the first things you need to know in math is that a line stands for a perimeter, a boundary. Many kids who attempt mazes on paper draw right through the lines. They don't see the lines as an obstruction. You can develop awareness of this convention by showing your child the boundaries that keep a player from straying off the path. As with all mathematical concepts, this is best learned physically; first with the whole body, then moving gradually to graphic representation.

Moving Ahead

Take a game that your child plays physically—baseball, for example—and suggest that your child work with you to create a board game out of it. Use a large sheet of poster board to create the board, and improvise tokens and other playing pieces.

Helpful Hint

Does your child know the way to school, to McDonald's, to the subway? Ask her to draw the way for you. Talk about the path she draws, discuss its features, and talk about alternative routes. Move ahead to Activity 28: Amazin' Game.

28 Amazin' Game

All the world's a maze.
I paraphrase Shakespeare to make the point
that most of us are trying to find our way.

You'll Need pages from newspapers or magazines; marker; pencil

Before You Begin Give your child plenty of experiences walking, leading the way to the park or to a friend's home, and playing board games that require staying on a path. Also see Activity 27: On the Road to Somewhere.

What to Do

1 Lay a sheet of newspaper between you and your child on a table.

2 Draw a circle with a marker in the margin on your side of the paper. Say, "This is where I'm going to start from."

3 Hand your child the marker. Ask him to draw a circle in the margin on his side of the paper to show where he wants you to finish.

4 Use a pencil to draw a path to the other side of the newspaper, where your child's finishing mark is drawn. Tell him the rules: you can't stay in the margins only, and you can't draw through any lines or type.

5 Talk about what you're thinking about and doing as you draw your path. "I'm moving around this column now. Here's a photograph to avoid. Then I'll move between these two lines . . ."

6 Choose another sheet of newspaper, and ask your child to draw the path this time.

Follow-up Activity Try all sorts of different newspaper and magazine pages. Draw conclusions with your child about which pages are the most difficult, and which are simpler, because of particular obstacles.

Mazes require a special kind of problem solving. You have to track along the open space with your eyes in order to find the best way through each maze. How far will you look ahead before drawing? What happens when you hit a blind alley? All of this requires thinking ahead, forming a strategy, and understanding that lines and type represent impenetrable walls.

Mazes are two-dimensional representations of space, and as such they are found on the entrance and placement exams for many schools. Your child needs practice with mazes of all kinds.

Moving Ahead

Use a heavy black marker to draw mazes for your child on white paper. Copy your maze so that your child can experiment with solving it in different ways. This builds flexibility and confidence, and lessens the pressure to get it right the first time.

Helpful Hints

- Find more mazes in children's magazines or coloring books. Make copies of these, too, so that your child can find all the different solutions.
- *Marvelous Mazes* by Juliet and Charles Snape is a book of pictorial mazes. In "Escape from the Castle," for instance, your child must use his eyes or a finger to follow a path through stairways, doors, and turrets.

29 Hats On!

Helps develop: *understanding of properties of shapes and structures, analyzing the relationship between form and function*

When I tried this activity in a workshop, we came up with more than fifty hats in an hour's time!

You'll Need
newspaper; large sheets of newsprint or drawing paper; scissors

Before You Begin
Try folding paper with your child. Introduce her to the idea that paper can be folded to create paper airplanes, boxes, or envelopes.

What to Do

1 Say, "I wonder if we can make a hat out of these pieces of paper?"

2 With your child, experiment with folding and draping the paper. See what you can come up with. Talk about what you're doing and thinking, and encourage your child to do the same. Ask her to explain hat ideas that she comes up with. "What made you think of that?" or "Oh, I see. You're folding the newspaper into a big triangle."

3 Talk about these amazing qualities of paper—that a big piece can be folded into a smaller object, that paper is flexible, foldable, cuttable, pastable.

Follow-up Activity

Here are some suggestions for making paper hats. Try them with your child. See if they give you new ideas about making hats.

● Use a paper plate. Draw a line along the fluted rim of the plate, about 2 inches (5 cm) in. Draw an animal shape from that line toward the center of the plate: a bunny head, for instance. Cut around the shape and the rim. Fold the shape upward. The rim forms the hat band.

- Cut an oval on a sheet of cardboard, at least 9 inches across. Cut out the center of the oval, making one end of the rim wider than the other. This is the beak of the visor.

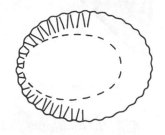

- Use an origami book to find more hat-folding ideas.

What's Happening

You're experimenting with the area of a piece of paper, an area that can be reorganized into a different shape for a given purpose. The concept is similar to figuring out how many Lego blocks are needed to make a house, to assessing how much fabric is required to make a shirt, to estimating how many yards of sod are needed to cover your lawn. The great thing about paper folding is that it's reversible; whatever you've fashioned can be unfolded into the sheet of paper it originally was. Making things, for a child, can seem like magic until she sees the process that goes into the creations.

Moving Ahead

Make hats for dolls or stuffed animals instead of for yourselves. How much paper will your child need to make a smaller hat of the right size?

Helpful Hint

Consult an origami book for ideas for ways to fold one small square of paper into many different animals; it's an interesting education in how an artist creates various forms with paper.

30 Parquet Play

Have you ever wished you could create your own floor tile pattern or rearrange the one you have? Rest assured it takes plenty of understanding of shape and area—the kind of understanding your child (and you) will get from working with parquet blocks.

Helps develop: awareness of patterns, properties and attributes of shapes, reversibility of patterns, ordering skills

You'll Need construction paper; scissors; pencil; patterns for triangles, squares, circles, diamonds, and other shapes

Before You Begin Make a set of parquet blocks by tracing the shapes below and cutting them from construction paper. Cut each shape from only one color, so that all triangles, for example, are green. Have your child work with you to create the set. Then let him explore them, arranging and rearranging to his heart's delight.

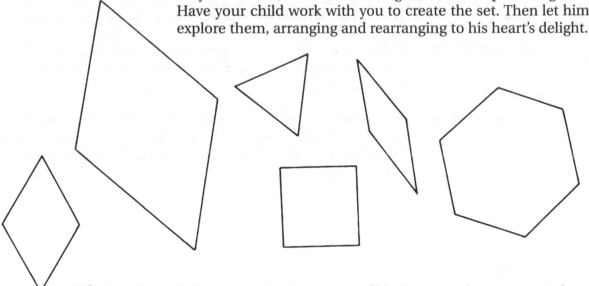

What to Do

1 Lay out a simple pattern of blocks: triangle, square, circle.

2 Invite your child to replicate your pattern.

3 Ask your child to make a pattern for you to copy. As you replicate the pattern, voice your thoughts: "Okay, this triangle goes next to the diamond. Then a circle goes next to the diamond." Use directional words: *above, below, right, left,* and so on. Use correct vocabulary to name the shapes.

4 Now re-create your original simple pattern. Say, "I wonder if we can do this again, *backward*." Talk through the process of reversing the pattern. "Okay, this has a triangle on the left. I'll put my triangle on the right." You're creating a mirror image of your child's pattern.

5 Experiment together with reversing patterns. Make a game of setting up patterns for each other to replicate backward.

Follow-up Activities

- Have your child record your activities on paper by tracing the shapes. Talk about what happens when you draw on paper (the shapes become static, no longer movable).

- Ask your child how many different patterns are possible with just three or four pieces. Work together to come up with variations. Keep track on paper, if you want.

What's Happening

Numbers go up and down, math operations go forward *(addition, multiplication) and backward (subtraction, division). A child begins to understand reversibility at a young age, when he experiences going somewhere and returning; whatever he saw last on the way to Grandma's is the first thing he passes on the way back. This pattern extends to numbers; but before your child can understand this fully, he needs experience manipulating and reversing patterns with concrete objects.*

Moving Ahead

Use several parquet blocks as counters. Ask your child to count out a number (say, three), and see what happens when you add two more. Say, "I wonder what happens if you take two away?" Experience with adding to and removing from a group of objects will help your child see the reversibility of addition and subtraction.

Helpful Hint

Use a computer drawing program to create pictures, write names, or design patterns. Then copy the picture, and flop it, using the tool that reverses. (In Aldus Freehand, it's called the reflector.) What's the result? Experiment with reversing many different designs.

PART THREE

Patterns and Relationships

What comes next? What's that? What happens if I change this? This section is about patterns that can be observed, created, copied, and extended; and about relationships between objects that can be studied, manipulated, recorded, and shared.

Yes, the focus of these activities is mathematical. But a key to every one of them is *doing* them. The activities call for seeing, hearing, feeling, moving around, and exploring through body and language.

Make these activities your own—and your child's own. You'll begin to see patterns and relationships everywhere you go.

31 Shoes in a Row

Helps develop: sorting, sequencing, and recognition of attributes

*How many ways can a pile of shoes be arranged?
Don't ask! Just provide your child with the shoes
(the boots beside the door will do fine) and stand back.*

You'll Need shoes

Before You Begin Let the shoes get good and mixed up. This may happen at your house without your trying!

What to Do

1 Draw your child's attention to the shoes. "Look at those shoes! What a mess! I'm going to fix them up." Then arrange them in a row against the wall, in any order you choose.

2 As you work, talk about what you're doing. "I'm putting Daddy's shoe with Daddy's shoe . . . Matthew's shoe with Matthew's shoe . . . Your shoe with your shoe."

3 Let your child get involved. Back off from your shoe arranging, and watch your child. Comment on what she does with quiet encouragement. "Hey, that's interesting. You put the biggest shoes on this end. Then a littler shoe, a littler shoe, an even littler shoe." Or, "Hmmm. A mish-mash pattern. Daddy's shoe next to Matthew's, then Mom's, then Matthew's."

4 That's it. Leave the shoes as your child arranged them. Listen as she shows her accomplishment to another family member.

Follow-up Activity Make shoe arranging a part of your routine. Your child doesn't have to do it every time you do, but she can be called on to give ideas or to say what she thinks of your arrangement. Note that changes are always "different," never wrong or strange.

What's Happening   Your child is examining a group of objects that are the same in some ways (they're all shoes) and different in others (size, color, fabric, style). She learns about these similarities and differences through looking, touching, and manipulating the shoes. She may say to herself, "Both these shoes are Daddy's. This shoe is bigger than that one." This ability to compare objects, place them in groups according to attributes, and create patterns, is fundamental to math. First graders will often be asked to spot patterns, describe them, and add to a sequence appropriately.

By the end of kindergarten, children are expected to be able to group objects by one or more attributes or characteristics. And children entering kindergarten are often asked to say which object in a group of four or more doesn't belong. By encouraging your child to explore a pile of objects and to talk about them, you give her important experience in grouping and in verbalizing her ideas.

Moving Ahead   Provide a bucket of shells, Lego blocks, buttons, or nuts. Your child may group things by color, size, or shape, may form them into patterns or lines, may put them into containers or assign them roles in a play she's acting out.

Helpful Hint   Help your child determine places to keep her toys, crayons, cars, and other things, but encourage her to determine for herself the order they go in. When it's cleanup time, you can say, "Time to put the cars back under the desk. I wonder how you'll line them up this time?"

32 Cats and Dogs

Words and objects make patterns, too, and their patterns may be easier to see than those in numbers.

You'll Need
twenty or so objects: ten of one kind, ten of another. Small plastic animals work nicely, but you can use anything from bottle caps to sheets of colored paper.

Before You Begin
Gather your objects together and put them in a box or bag.

What to Do

1 Sit beside your child. Hold the box or bag in your lap so that your child cannot see inside it.

2 Look inside. Say, "Hmm! Look here!" Pull out a plastic animal, perhaps a cat, and stand it in front of your child. Ask, "What's this?"

3 Look into your bag again. "Ahh!" Pull out a dog and stand it beside the cat. Ask, "What's this?"

4 Pull out another cat. Ask your child what it is. "Is it the same as the first cat? No? What's different about it? Different color?"

5 Go on setting out animals: cat, dog, cat, dog, cat, dog, cat.

6 Now say, "Do you want to finish the pattern?" Hand the bag to your child.

7 See what your child sets out. Is it a dog?

8 Have your child continue laying out animals until the bag is empty, and then recap what the pattern is. You might say, "Hey, look. After every cat comes a dog. And after every dog comes a cat!"

Follow-up Activities
- Use other patterns as you lay out the animals: cat, cat, cat, dog . . .
- Take turns being the leader.
- Add different animals to the bag: ten pigs, for example.

What's Happening This is a very concrete activity that requires your child to study a pattern while focusing his attention on just one item at a time. As you speak the names of the items in the pattern, you help your child to hear the rhythm, too.

Moving Ahead Talk patterns to your child. Instead of laying out actual objects, just say: "I'm thinking of a cat and a dog. And another dog, and a cat. Cat, dog, dog, cat. What do you think comes next?"

Helpful Hint To keep track of patterns you've done before, ask your child to draw the animals in their patterns. Keep a little book of patterns. Eventually your child might consider creating patterns on paper *first*. Then you can follow his drawing to create the pattern with the objects.

33 Is It or Isn't It?

*Only the keeper of the toy box
knows for sure what's in there.*

You'll Need the contents of a toy box, book shelf, or junk drawer

Before You Begin Do this activity while you're straightening a drawer. This activity starts on the same level as Activity 31: Shoes in a Row and involves similar concepts.

What to Do

1 Lay out the toys, books, or junk on the floor or a tabletop. Sit beside your child.

2 Ask your child to find an object that has a given attribute. Say, for example:
   - "Can you find something hard?"
   - "I spy something green."
   - "I wonder if there is anything with wheels in this pile."

3 Keep it open-ended, discussing each object your child suggests. Take turns picking up objects that have the attribute you suggested and placing them in a group together until you and your child agree that there are no more objects with that attribute in the pile.

4 Replace the group of objects in the pile and mix them up.

5 Ask your child to name another attribute to search for, and again take turns placing the appropriate items together.

Follow-up Activities

- "But, wait!" you say. "That green thing was in the hard pile, too! Can something be hard *and* green?" Of course the answer is yes, but rather than asking your child initially to search out objects with two attributes, you've helped her reach her own conclusion. Now ask, "Is there anything else here that's hard and green?" The search starts anew.

- Another way of adding an attribute is to make your request a negative. "Can you find something that's not hard?" True, all you're really asking for is something soft—one attribute. For your child, *not hard* is two attributes. It involves a higher level of thinking. Only use negatives when your child is successful with at least two attributes.

What's Happening

Classification—grouping according to attribute—is one of the vital conceptual activities that children must master to understand math and even reading. In order to read, children must be able to differentiate between straight and curved lines, to see patterns in the formation of a letter, and to understand the purpose of punctuation and spacing. To do math, children must identify numbers, functions, shapes, lines, and other things simply on the strength of their recognizable attributes. Give your child a lot of practice with sorting and classifying objects of all kinds, using one to four attributes. Note that one and two attributes at a time is the limit for most young children, three and four coming when the child reaches a higher level of understanding.

Moving Ahead

Try Activity 34: Junk Drawer Jumbalaya, which takes classification into higher realms by asking children to figure out the attributes by which objects are grouped.

Helpful Hint

Watch what you say when you direct your child to do something. When you say, "Get your boots, put on your hat, and wait by the door," you're giving three directions each with its own attribute. It's too difficult for most young children to deal with. Make a chart, using adding machine tape to draw or write reminders of what's required to go outdoors, or give your child at most two directions at a time.

34 Junk Drawer Jumbalaya

34 Junk Drawer Jumbalaya

Helps develop: *identification of attributes, sorting, classifying*

If you look closely enough, everything has something in common with everything else.

You'll Need the junk drawer in your house (the longer the junk has been around, the better) *or* a toy chest *or* a sewing box

Before You Begin Dump out a pile of stuff. Eliminate anything that's potentially dangerous and allow your child to explore. Then ask your child to pick out about ten items, and pick out ten items yourself. Do this activity after your child has attained most of the concepts from Activity 33: Is It or Isn't It?

What to Do

1 Tell your child, "I'm looking at all of these things to see if I can find two things that go together."

2 Separate two objects from the pile and lay them side by side before your child. Start off with a pair whose common attributes may be the most obvious thing about them: for example, two objects that have screws, or two that have wheels.

3 Ask your child to note the things you pick out and try to determine what characteristic they have in common.

4 Accept all logical answers, saying, "That's an interesting notion," or "You're right! They are both blue."

5 If your child can't come up with the attribute your objects have in common, search the pile for another object that also shares this attribute. "Here's another member of the group."

6 In the end, if your child still hasn't thought of an attribute that links your objects, tell him what it is. Then work together to find more objects from the pile that share that attribute. Tell your child your thoughts as you look at and touch the objects to determine if they share the attribute.

Follow-up Activities
- Move on to less obvious attributes, such as texture or purpose.
- Turn the tables. Have your child select a group of two or three objects and continue to add to them while you try to figure out an attribute they share.

What's Happening

When your child hears you describe your process for finding attributes, he'll think about his own process, adding new ideas about what constitutes an attribute. For each object, your child goes down a mental list of attributes to find a match. This requires a careful analysis of attributes and the ability to name them. In mathematics, sets are classes of objects that share a single attribute. When you find all the objects in a drawer that are blue, you establish a set of blue objects. This is an important concept of math that is built on more in Activity 37: Set 'Em Up.

Moving Ahead

Tell your child that the group you have selected has two or three common attributes. Ask your child to figure out what they might be.

Helpful Hint

Catalogs are interesting in that they often group objects that have a similar theme: firefighter costumes with stuffed Dalmatian toys and fire engines. Browse through a catalog or two with your child and ask him to suggest why things are grouped as they are. Is it random? Are they baby toys? Men's shoes? Socks and stockings? Outdoor games? Crafts with beads?

35 People Pieces

*Will everyone with blue jeans
and blue eyes please stand up?*

You'll Need   index cards; scissors; paste; old magazines

Before You Begin   Use your child's dolls or action figures as the subject of a classifying activity such as Activity 33: Is It or Isn't It? Once she's gotten the hang of it, move to this activity with its flat, two-dimensional representations of people instead of three-dimensional representations.

What to Do   **1** Work with your child to select and cut out ten to twenty pictures of people from magazines. Each cutout person should fit on an index card.

2 Paste each cutout person on the blank side of an index card.

3 Spread the cards out on a flat surface, face down.

4 Invite your child to choose two cards and turn them face up. Ask your child to find one, two, or three (depending on her level) attributes that the people pictured have in common. Your child might focus on activities the people are pursuing, or age, sex, appearance, facial expression, clothing, surroundings, or anything else that comes to mind.

5 Place your child's two cards in front of you and turn over a third card. Suggest one, two, or three attributes that all three have.

Follow-up Activities   • Take turns turning over two cards, or add a person to the group each time.

• Make a stack of cards with one-word cues printed on them: *tall, smiling, young, busy* . . . Ask your child to find all the people who fit each word cue.

What's Happening *Rather than finding like attributes of random objects, this activity requires taking a closer look at "objects" with the same basic form and the shared attribute of being humans. Children are required to look closer. Because all members of this set of objects have certain characteristics—they all have hair, skin, gender, clothing, facial expression—the challenge comes in finding more specific similarities and differences.*

Moving Ahead Line up the people in a pattern and see if your child can identify the pattern. For example: male, female, female, male; long hair, short hair, no hair; smiling, not smiling.

Helpful Hint You and your child can make another set of people pieces by drawing a basic paper doll without hair or features, copying it several times, and decorating each doll in different ways.

36 Line 'Em Up

Helps develop: *understanding of seriation, use of graphic representation of concepts, use of language to compare*

*"Okay, now," says the four-year-old to the boxes.
"Which one of you's the biggest?"*

You'll Need five or more cardboard boxes that are notably different in size but all small enough to fit on a sheet of paper (jar lids work well too); a sheet of cardboard; white glue; paper; pencil; index card

Before You Begin Explore the idea of placing objects in a series with your child through Activity 31: Shoes in a Row. Once he has that down, try this higher-level version of that activity.

What to Do

1 Let your child play with and explore the boxes.

2 Talk with your child about the differences between the boxes. Suggest that he set them up in a line, and talk about his method of doing this. Is the pattern random? Are the boxes set up in a series from largest to smallest?

3 Ask your child which setup he likes the best. Suggest that he can keep this setup by gluing the boxes onto a sheet of cardboard. Hand over the glue.

4 Talk about the finished product. "Why is this one second in line?" Repeat the words that your child uses to show how each box is different from the others: "Oh, I see—because it's bigger than that one but smaller than the rest."

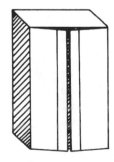

Follow-up Activities

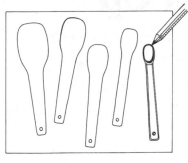

- Ask your child to think of another way to show the size of something on paper. Remind him (if necessary) that tracing shows the outline of a size and shape. The finished product will be a series of traced objects, rather than glued-down objects.

- Give your child an index card or a slip of note paper. Ask him, "Did you want to remember how you lined up the dolls? How could you do it without tracing?" Let your child come up with his own strategy for recording his series. He may think of drawing little dolls, or of coming up with a symbolic representation, such as stars, each one bigger than the last, or he may write the doll's name in its position in the lineup.

What's Happening

The first job—lining up objects—involves placing material things in a series. The second job involves transferring them physically to paper—a step toward representing them on paper. Once you've moved the topic to paper, it's a simple step to show the series of objects without them physically being there—and then another step from showing the objects at actual size to representing them symbolically. Through these activities (the follow-ups will follow over a course of months or years if you start with a young child), your child passes from concrete to representational math—the kind of math that he will deal with in large part as he moves ahead in school.

Moving Ahead
Move from seriating objects held in the hand to larger objects such as buildings, trees, and people. Point out a group of buildings or other large objects to your child and say, "I wonder which of those is the tallest? Smallest? Widest?"

Helpful Hint
Look everywhere for objects of different sizes that your child can use to paste down or trace. Junk drawers are a great resource (batteries, rubber bands, and magnets) as are stationery stores (stickers, labels, and erasers) and hardware stores (keys, nails, screws, and washers).

37 Set 'Em Up

Helps develop:
concept of sorting,
graphic skills repre-
senting classification,
categorizing skills,
fine motor skills

What floats?
What sinks?

You'll Need two cake pans full of water, various objects (things that float and don't float); paper; pencil; scissors

Before You Begin Do this very basic activity once your child can match objects according to color, function, or some other attribute.

What to Do
1 Ask your child, "I wonder how we can find out which of these things floats?" See what your child comes up with. She may make predictions or simply start trying to float one of the objects.

2 Move on to the other objects. Have your child try floating these.

3 Designate one pan for floating objects and one for non-floating objects, and let your child put each object into the appropriate pan.

4 Suggest a way to record the grouping. Use the paper to help your child trace the outline of each cake pan. Cut out on the lines. Ask your child to place each object onto the appropriate cake pan outline and trace it there.

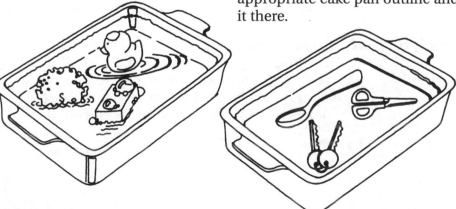

Follow-up Activity   Try grouping a set of objects found outdoors according to whether they're alive or not alive. Create a third category for objects you and your child aren't sure of.

What's Happening   When your child knows that something floats, she knows that it has one attribute. To know that another object does not float, she must identify two attributes: the characteristic of floating and the negative of it—that the attribute is not there. Bringing assorted objects into the question requires the child to analyze each of them and group them according to attributes. The use of the cake pans adds another aspect: the creation of sets with labels that may be filled or left empty. What if everything floats? Then you have one set with a number of members and another set with none.

Moving Ahead   What if something has a floating part and a nonfloating part, such as a plastic troll with hair? Suggest that your child think of a way to show how the sets are combined. (On paper, this requires intersecting the outlines of the cake pans.)

Helpful Hint   Do more work with sets by taking on Activity 38: Loops and Hoops.

38 Loops and Hoops

H *elps develop:* *sorting, naming attributes, grouping by set, understanding inclusion (intersection) in sets*

A bag of groceries is chock-full of opportunities for getting into math.

You'll Need a bag of groceries; a ball of string; scissors

Before You Begin Unload a bag of groceries onto a countertop or table. Put away anything that's perishable.

What to Do

1 Invite your child to sort out the groceries.

2 Watch your child. Talk to him about his groupings. What would you call this group? And this? And this? What would you call the whole pile?

3 Make several large loops of string (1 to 2 feet [30 to 60 cm] round).

4 Ask your child to use each loop to separate one group from the others. For example, one loop might hold brown things: bread, potatoes, raisins, peanut butter. The other might hold green things: peas, pickles, cans of tuna fish. Note that initially you should loop in only two categories (sets). Some objects may fall outside the loops.

Follow-up Activities

• Look for an attribute that some items in the two different sets have in common. For example, with the list above, you might say, "What about rectangles? What could you do with them?" See what your child suggests: Another loop? Dividing the whole group by shape instead? What if you wanted to show green, brown, *and* rectangles? Move the loops so that they intersect. In the intersection, invite your child to place the objects that are rectangular: bread, raisins in little boxes, a bag of peas.

- Get hold of photographs of each member of your family. Refer to Activity 15: Take a Vote for ideas about polling family members. Instead of placing stickers on a graph to show where each person stands, use photographs and your loops of string. Begin with one piece of data, such as gender. Divide the family into two groups by gender. Then ask another question, such as, "Do you like lima beans?" Figure out together how to show both gender and preferences through intersecting loops.

What's Happening

Laying objects out in groups with a loop of string to define them helps children to see the categories they've created as sets of objects with something in common. But any object has many attributes, and a group of objects is naturally sorted in a great variety of ways. By finding many ways to group a bag of groceries and creating several intersections of categories or sets, you'll help your child to see things more flexibly, to identify many different attributes in single objects, and to understand a new way of recording his findings.

Moving Ahead

Ask your child to keep a record of the loop sets you create by drawing them on paper and labeling them.

Helpful Hint

On index cards, paste labels from your groceries, or have your child draw pictures of items. Use these cards to graph this selection of groceries. Decide on a category, such as vegetables. Line up the vegetable cards, one beside the other, on the floor or table. Then line up the nonvegetables. Which are there more of? Which set has less?

39 Scribble Scrimmage

Helps develop:
creating patterns,
analysis of pattern

A scribble is a random drawing; a scrimmage is a meeting of minds. Put your mind together with your child's to create a beautiful patterned picture.

You'll Need   paper; black felt-tip pen; colored markers or crayons

Before You Begin   Invite your child to create a piece of artwork with you. Gather together the writing materials, and, using the black pen, demonstrate how to make the scribble: a large, loopy tangle of lines with many small sections for coloring in and no open lines.

What to Do

1 Decide who's going to make the scribble. Scribble away, using the black pen to cover much of the space on the paper.

2 As you (or your child) scribble, talk about what makes a pattern: dots, stripes, and plaids.

3 Ask your child to help you fill the sections of the scribble with one pattern per section using the colored markers or crayons. As you work, talk about what you're doing: "I'm making red and white stripes. Next I think I'll make a rainbow." Continue working until the scribble is filled in with patterns, or until you or your child gets tired. (If this happens, put it aside for another time. A good scribble can take days to complete.)

4 When you're finished, talk about all the different patterns you and your child created. How many striped patterns are there? How many dots?

5 Proudly display your cooperative artistic effort! Encourage your child to describe the patterns to interested parties.

Follow-up Activity   Look around for patterns similar to the ones you and your child included in your Scribble Scrimmage. Point them out to your child.

What's Happening   *It's one thing to observe patterns everywhere you go: spiderwebs in the corners, ripples on a lake, steps and window frames and lines on paper. It's another thing to recall those patterns and replicate them on paper. As a child draws a pattern, she must think about what comes next in the sequence and, indeed, whether there's a pattern in what she's doing at all. When you work side by side, you have the opportunity to model how patterns are created.*

Don't miss the opportunity to goof up your pattern and let your child know about it. For children to learn to be risk takers, parents need to be fallible. Don't put yourself down, but don't be the expert either. Ask your child, "Does this look like a pattern to you? Oops, you're right. I should have made that dot green instead of red."

Moving Ahead   Make a pattern within a pattern. Instead of scribbling, create a large grid like a checkerboard. Inside each grid, make other, smaller grids (graph paper is helpful in this). With your child, come up with a multitude of ways to create grid patterns within the grid.

Helpful Hint   Is your child having trouble getting started on a pattern? Ask her to copy one of the patterns on her clothing: plaid, corduroy, ribbing, denim twill, a floral or dotted fabric all have patterns that are there for the taking.

40 Edging a Pillow

*What more could a child want than
a pillow for his head, made by his own hand,
with your guidance?*

Helps develop: *fine-motor skills, using a pattern, tracing, the process of sewing*

You'll Need
burlap or needlepoint canvas; needlepoint needle; heavy yarn; newspaper; scissors; white muslin; tracing pencil; pinking shears; fabric crayons, paint, or markers; pins; needle and thread; old panty hose

Before You Begin
Using a square of burlap or needlepoint canvas, the needle-point needle, and the heavy yarn, teach your child how to sew a running stitch by going in and out of the open holes in the fabric.

What to Do

1 Plan a pillow to decorate your child's bed, cushion his bottom, or grace a favorite chair. Decide together the size and shape of the pillow. Cut a sheet of newspaper to the shape and size wanted. This will be the template for the pillow.

2 Have your child trace the newspaper template onto a double layer of muslin with the tracing pencil.

3 Help your child cut the muslin with pinking shears, cutting through both layers together.

4 Separate the muslin. Have your child use the fabric crayons, markers, or paint to decorate the pillow's face (and also the back, if he wants). Follow the manufacturer's directions for setting these decorations permanently into the fabric.

5 Pin the pillow face to the back.

6 Guide your child to sew a running stitch along three edges of the pillow.

7 Remove all pins.

8 Have your child stuff the pillow with old panty hose (they're cheap, available, and washable).

9 Finish the pillow by sewing a running stitch along the fourth side.

Follow-up Activity Encourage your child to show the finished product to others and to explain the process he used to make it.

What's Happening *As he works on this project (which should take several days at least, and can be done anywhere), your child must consider size, perimeter, shape, function, design, color, pattern, and placement of stitches. This is just one example of how a craft activity helps build a multitude of concepts. Your child will estimate how much yarn he'll need, how many stitches it will take to reach the corner, and how much stuffing is required to fill the pillow. He'll try to keep his stitching a regular distance from the edge, and he'll try to make his stitches consistent. As he finishes, he will have achieved many goals that contribute to his overall understanding of the concepts that underlie his actions, estimations, and calculations. The process will also illustrate that one step builds on another to reach the goal. That will be a key concept for later equation solving.*

Moving Ahead Have your child design and sew a dashiki, a pullover top that can serve as an apron or smock. Cut a length of fabric that is double the measurement from your child's neck to his hips. Use pinking shears to cut a hole for the head. Have the child sew the sides up (leaving arm holes) and decorate it.

Helpful Hint Extend your child's understanding of the basic process of sewing a pillow by having him direct you as you make beanbags on a sewing machine. The child's job? To cut squares of fabric for you to sew on three sides; to fill the bags with beans; to sew up the fourth edge by hand; to create a game for the beanbags.

41 Button Collage

In a favorite Laura Ingalls Wilder story, two little girls make their baby sister a button string. They happily string and restring the buttons, taking delight in every available button. I'm willing to bet that buttons hold just as much fascination for your child today.

Helps develop: sorting, fine-motor skills, covering area, assessing attributes, grouping

You'll Need buttons of many shapes and sizes; sturdy fabric; pinking shears; needle and thread

Before You Begin Place the buttons in a box or can and give them to your child to explore and sort. Discuss the buttons: "What fabric or piece of clothing would this one look good on?" "Let me tell you about the shirt this one came off, long ago." "How old do you think this button might be?" Have your child make a button string or two, simply threading buttons onto a needle and thread. Have her sew a button with large holes onto a scrap of fabric. Sew another kind of button on. Let the child sew until she's fairly competent. This will give her necessary experience with the materials. When she's ready for more, move on to this sewing project.

What to Do 1 Suggest to your child that she can use these buttons to make a button collage. She can sew the buttons onto a piece of fabric and keep it, hang it, make it into something else, or give it away. Have her choose a piece of fabric. Cut it with pinking shears to keep the edges from fraying.

2 Thread the needle, double the thread, and knot it. This will keep the thread from slipping out of the needle.

3 Let your child choose the placement, but guide her in the sewing on of each button. Point out to her that different buttons require different sewing methods.

4 Discuss your child's choice and placement of the buttons. Why are these two close together? Which one do you like best? How do you decide which one comes next?

Follow-up Activities

- Use the finished product as the face of a pillow. Sew another square of fabric to it around three edges, stuff, and close.

- Use the finished product to make a bag. Sew another square of fabric to it on three sides and attach a ribbon strap.

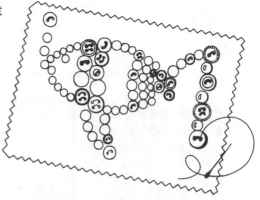

What's Happening

There are so many types of buttons, so many methods of sewing them on, so many colors, textures, sizes, shapes, and materials. Each of these attributes provides a basis for sorting and comparing, choosing and classifying. Combine the exploration of buttons with a sewing project and you add experience using hands to acquire skills as well as concepts.

Moving Ahead

Have your child replace the buttons on a cardigan or shirt. Take the garment along to a sewing supply store, and guide your child as she tries out different buttons, fitting them into the holes. She'll have to decide how many she needs, choose their colors, and be involved in paying for them, even before she goes home to work with you at sewing them on. Of course, the old buttons go into the button box for future use.

Helpful Hint

If you're no expert button sewer yourself, consult the clerk in a sewing store for a demonstration, or pick up a book on sewing at the library. Study and practice together, and you'll give your child another life skill: how to find the information you need to get something done.

42 Slap Jack

*This card game is a "hit"
with even the youngest child.*

Helps develop: identifying members of a set, matching symbols to actions, scanning to find characteristics

You'll Need   a deck of playing cards

Before You Begin   Lay the face cards from a regular deck of cards on the table. Talk about them with your child. Compare the kings, queens, and jacks. Compare each king to the other kings, each queen to the other queens, and each jack to the other jacks. Talk about one-eyed and two-eyed jacks. Look at the nonface cards, too. What are their numbers and symbols?

What to Do   1 Divide the cards into two equal piles, one for you, one for your child, or deal the cards in the whole deck out one by one.

2 Each of you places your cards in front of you, face down.

3 Each player takes the top card in his or her pile and places it, face up, in the center of the table. If either player's card is a jack, the first person to slap it wins all the cards in the center of the table. If both cards are jacks, the first person to hit one of them wins the cards. If neither card is a jack, both players take the next card on their pile and place it face up in the center, continuing this way until a jack appears.

4 Play continues until one person has no cards left or until players are ready to stop.

Follow-up Activity   Choose another card to be "it." Play Slap Four, Slap Ace, or whatever.

What's Happening

In order to play this game, your child must be able to quickly discern jacks. He must note each jack's attributes in a flash, and recognize that jacks are the only set of cards that require action. Eventually, he'll figure out that there are four jack cards and begin to strategize accordingly.

Sometimes kids goof, hitting the wrong face card. Stop, back up, and talk about the characteristics of the jack card. Even children who have a firm idea of what a jack is will sometimes start hitting everything. It may seem as if they're trying to win by overreacting. What's happening, more likely, is that they're getting stuck and forgetting the set. Remind them of what they're looking for, or let the game end and play something that brings the heart rate down: Try matching cards, building a card house, playing a game of predicting which color card will come up next: black or red.

Moving Ahead

Raise the level of this game by playing Bow to the King. This game requires an active response to all the face cards. To win cards, players must be the first to slap jacks, say "Good morning, Ma'am" to the queens, and bow to the kings.

Helpful Hint

As with all materials, give your child ample opportunity to explore and play with the cards. Through sorting, shuffling, and arranging, your child will get a better picture of what every card, denomination, and suit looks like.

43 Half 'n' Half

Helps develop:
understanding of symmetry, pattern recognition

When your child is faced with half a picture, she fills in the space with clues from the existing pattern.

You'll Need old magazines; scissors; paste; drawing paper; pencil; crayons and/or markers

Before You Begin Make a pile of several simple, graphic pictures from a magazine and cut each in half. Ask your child to look through the pile to find the other half of each picture. Talk about the clues the child used to match up the halves.

What to Do 1 Present your child with a group of three picture halves. Invite her to choose one to finish.

2 Ask your child to glue the picture half onto drawing paper.

3 Invite your child to draw the other half of the picture so that it connects up with the cutout half.

4 Talk about the project with your child as she works, if she's willing. If not, talk about it when she's finished. Some possible discussion points: What decisions did she have to make? What clues did she use? What's the same in one half as in the other half? How did she know to make it the same or different?

Follow-up Activity Invite your child to try completing another picture half. What did she learn the first time that can help her this time?

What's Happening

The heart of this project is the understanding of symmetry—one half of something being the mirror image of the other—or asymmetry, the flip side, in which two sides don't match. A child gets clues as to whether something should be symmetrical or asymmetrical by studying the pattern set in the first half of the picture and using prior knowledge of the subject in the picture. For example, if the cutout shows half a person's face, the child knows to make the other half symmetrically. If the cutout shows the front end of a car, the child's experience of cars tells him to make the back end of the car to complete the picture. Much of math understanding involves being able to look at numbers, lines, or shapes, and determine whether they match up, or are equal.

Moving Ahead

Much visual humor comes from the unexpected. You can do the Half 'n' Half activity with a slight twist: Take a small notebook. Cut the pages in half crosswise. Have your child use the top half-pages to make drawings of a variety of top halves of animals and people and the bottom half-pages to draw a random assortment of the bottom halves of various creatures. The result is a booklet of odd combinations. Readers can attempt to match tops with bottoms or can create a bunch of silly critters.

Helpful Hint

Anno's Math Book by Mitsumasa Anno includes an illustrated discussion of what happens when half of something is put together with half of something else to make a new invention: a tray with wheels becomes a cart, a cane and an umbrella becomes an umbrella with a curved handle, and so on.

44 Paper Cutups

Reflections, negatives, flip sides—they're all big words for basic concepts that your child will love exploring with a very basic material: paper

Helps develop: identification of patterns, their reversibility and symmetry

You'll Need   paper; paint; scissors; hole puncher

Before You Begin   Fold a sheet of paper in half. Open it and have your child paint a design on the top half. Wait until the paint is partly dry. Then have your child fold the bottom half on top of the painted half and press down gently. Open, and you'll have a reverse copy of your child's design. This opens your child's eyes to the idea of symmetry and reversal.

What to Do

1 Fold a sheet of paper in half. Cut a very simple design in it, such as a half heart, similar to a lopsided C-shape. Be sure to cut through both folded sides.

2 Say, "I wonder what this will look like when it's opened up?" Invite your child to make a prediction.

3 Open the paper up and look at the shape. Talk about the two halves that work together to create the whole.

4 Now ask your child to fold a sheet of paper in half and make his own design with scissors.

5 Make many sheets of paper available to your child. Work with him to make an assortment of designs.

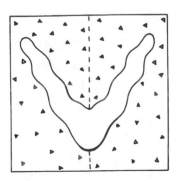

- Have your child fold his paper twice to make quadrants rather than halves. What sort of designs arise from doing this?
- Fold paper in half and invite your child to create a pattern with a hole puncher. Open it when he's through and talk about what makes the pattern symmetrical.

What's Happening

Reflection is part of every aspect of math, from geometric proofs to negative numbers, and the ability to understand the concept on a basic level is helpful to children. A pattern is recreated not only by following a continuous sequence, but also by reflecting and reversing the sequence from the center. This activity makes the fold in the paper that center; every other part of the pattern works outward. As your child works, he cuts both sides of the pattern at once. As he notices this, he'll begin to apply it to make more intricate shapes. An especially interesting version: cutting out one's name.

Moving Ahead

Suggest that your child trace a basic shape (a leaf, a toy, a hand) onto a folded sheet of black paper, then cut it out with the center of the shape at the fold. The resulting shape will be symmetrical: there will be a black leaf cutout, and a leaf-shaped space in the black paper from which the leaf was cut. Paste the cutout onto white paper and the space onto white paper as well. This shows the same shape in positive and negative form.

Helpful Hint

Make classic fold-out paper dolls. Fold a long strip of paper lengthwise and fold it accordion-fashion, making a fold about every 3 inches (8 cm). Cut one shape (it doesn't have to be paper dolls), making sure that some part of it extends to the sides of the panel. The result will be a string of your shape, one for each panel you folded.

45 Borderline Math

> *Helps develop:*
> *understanding of area and perimeter, creating and recognizing patterns, using shapes and sizes*

They say a picture is worth a thousand words. In this activity, creating a frame around a picture is worth a thousand math lessons.

You'll Need examples of borders, such as those found in wallpaper books, catalogs, picture books, and magazines, or on stationery, tiling, game boards, fabrics, or postage stamps; paper; pencil; crayons or markers; rubber stamps and ink

Before You Begin Zero in on a border that interests your child, or point out a border that interests you. Some children will spend more time drawing a border or frame for a drawing than they do on the drawing itself. If your child does this, she's already into this border activity!

What to Do
1 Talk with your child about what a certain border looks like. Note the colors, patterns, size, and shape.

2 Ask her questions about it. Does this border repeat itself? Where's the part that repeats? How long (how far can you move your finger along) before it starts to repeat?

3 Discuss ideas about why the border is there. Why, for instance, would you place a wallpaper border around the top of a wall or around the center? Why is the border of a tiled bathroom different from the rest of the wall or the floor? Why would an artist enclose an illustration in a border?

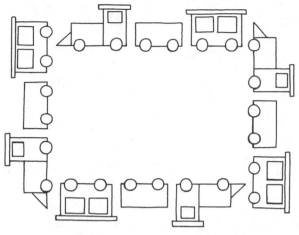

4 Ask your child if she'd like to make her own border. Invite her to select a picture she's already drawn to edge with a border. Or provide paper and drawing materials and have her draw a border without a picture. Give her a purpose, telling her that the border can frame a drawing later or can be used in a picture frame around a photograph.

5 Talk to your child about her work. Note her choice of color and pattern. Talk about the *repeat* (the length of the pattern before it repeats itself) of the pattern, if there is one.

Follow-up Activity Show your child how to use a rubber stamp or a stamp cut from a potato or an apple to create a repeating border. Point out that she can make the pattern more complicated by using two or more stamps.

What's Happening Your child is exploring the perimeter around a sheet of paper with her eyes and with her hands, as she finds out just how many figures or shapes it takes to create a border. As your child notices other borders, she gains understanding of how artists use shapes and colors to create patterns. If her border—either the one she studies or the one she makes—has a repeat, then she must do a careful analysis of the pattern to figure out how many of an element are required to cover a space.

Moving Ahead Make a study of the zillions of readily observable borders in the world. With your child, search out borders on building facades, on writing paper, on drinking glasses, and on other decorated objects. Take a sketchbook or camera along, and document these borders for a border book of your own.

Helpful Hint Paint stores frequently offer wallpaper books from discontinued lines, free of charge. It's fascinating to study the samples of wallpaper borders side by side with photographs showing how the border looks in a room. You might consider putting up a border in your child's room; some of them are made of material that hangs temporarily, so if your residence (or your child's taste) changes, the border can be taken down.

PART FOUR

Math Strategies

You've got a problem. How do you figure it out?

In your mind is a toolbox of past experiences, strategies, and techniques for unraveling a snarl and getting to the bottom of a puzzle. The activities in this section are designed to help your child develop his own toolbox. Use these games and experiences to help your child understand probability, develop problem-solving skills, and become more flexible in his thinking.

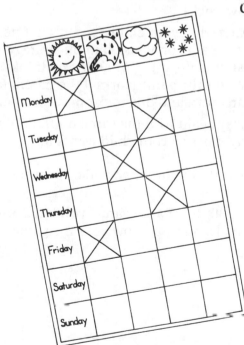

46 Rock Pile

This simple game brings laughs and forehead-smacking frustration, while teaching your child strategy and planning. It's fun for adults, too.

Helps develop: one-to-one correspondence, problem-solving strategy, basic addition, subtraction, multiplication, and division

You'll Need   a little pile of about ten rocks, paper clips, pennies, or beads; a tabletop or other flat surface (a book will do)

Before You Begin   Lay all the rocks out on the table, any way you like. Don't let them overlap.

What to Do

1 Tell your child that the object of this game is to take the last rock. The two of you will take turns. On each turn, you can each take one or two rocks.

2 Play the game. Watch what your child does. It's not necessary to talk about the game or advise him on strategy. If he asks you what he should do, ask, "What do *you* think?" It helps the child see how the game works if the parent takes two rocks on the first turn and one rock on the second.

3 Finish the game. Play again with the same number of rocks in the pile, as many times as your child wants to.

Follow-up Activities

- After a few rounds with that number, add or take away a few rocks.

- Expand to 20 rocks, 30, 40. Try the game with large objects: books, stuffed animals, buckets. How does the game change?

What's Happening Through this game your child will begin to grasp what a number really is. By playing this game, your child is seeing how many different ways a group of a certain number divides up into smaller portions. Such practice is helpful in understanding all the basic operations of math.

As your child plays, he must think ahead, strategize. This game, like tic-tac-toe and connect-the-dots, is fascinating for kids who haven't yet figured out and repeated each strategy hundreds of times. This kind of strategizing can't be taught.

Moving Ahead For an older child, move the game to paper. Draw ten or more dots on a page and play the game by circling the dots. (Use different colored pens, or a pencil and a pen.) You'll give your child important experience in moving from concrete objects to paper representation.

Helpful Hint The point of involving a child in competition is to help him learn to win *and* lose gracefully. A very competitive child may want to win every time. It's up to you how you handle this, but keep in mind: when you lose, you show him how to take a risk and lose with grace. On the other hand, if you go all out, you'll demonstrate something else: how to strategize. Each of these experiences is equally valuable.

47 Traffic Lights A-Go-Go

Helps develop:
understanding of
a technological pattern
and its relationship to
real objects, planning
and executing a math-
ematical survey, observ-
ing cause and effect

How does the light know to turn red?
What does it mean when it's yellow?
Why doesn't it always stay green?

You'll Need   a traffic intersection; paper and pencil; rubber stamp with a car on it (optional)

Before You Begin   Ask your child if he'd like to learn more about the traffic light at a nearby intersection. Most of the children I know show an interest in traffic lights. You might also use time spent waiting for a bus at an intersection to start this activity spontaneously.

What to Do

1 If your child hasn't already raised the issue, say, "I wonder how the traffic light decides to change." Talk it over. Your child may suggest that the light is mechanical and changes automatically. Say, "But how does it know *when* to change?" The conclusion may be reached that the light is on a timer. Wonder aloud, "How did the people who set it decide what time to make it change?"

2 Say, "I wonder how we can find out how many cars each red light is going to stop." Ask your child for suggestions.

3 Find a comfortable spot near the traffic light. Watch only one light pointing in one direction.

4 Turn your paper sideways. Write the numbers 1 through 10 at the bottom of the paper. These numbers represent the number of red lights you might watch through. Watch as many lights as your child wants.

5 Together, watch the cars that stop after the light turns red. For each car, make a mark (or a rubber stamp) beside the

number 1. Make the marks in a row, so that each light can be compared with the others.

6 Continue counting cars for each light until you have waited through each light. During the green lights, talk about what's going on. Why do the cars have to wait at the light? Which line of traffic seems to have the most cars? What is the purpose of this traffic light?

Follow-up Activities

- Talk with your child about how you could figure out whether the traffic flow changes at different times of day.
- Compare the traffic flow from the other direction or from the cross road.

What's Happening

By solving the problem with numbers, you're helping your child answer the question "Why does this light need to be here?" Taken on its own, as such things often are by young children, the light just sits there changing colors. This activity focuses attention on the cars whose motion is affected by the light, and leads to conclusions about the flow of traffic through that intersection. When your child counts cars that come to the light before it changes green, she's learning to measure time in a nonstandard way—key to the concept of understanding time.

Moving Ahead

Use what you've learned to conduct studies of other intersections, especially large ones with pedestrian WALK/DON'T WALK lights, left-turn signals, right-on-red, and so on. Talk about the traffic laws and how they affect the flow of traffic.

Helpful Hint

Play Red Light, Green Light with your child. Have your child stand on a starting line ten feet from you. Turn your back, close your eyes, and shout, "Green light!" Count quickly to ten. Your child must move toward you, trying to reach you and touch you before you get to ten, turn around, and shout, "Red light!" Your child must freeze before you turn. If you catch her moving, she has to go back. If you have several children playing, the first to reach you becomes the traffic light.

48 Oh, Waiter!

How many in your party?
Planning a meal can be a rich math adventure.

Helps develop: understanding of one-to-one correspondence, counting, understanding sets

You'll Need table-setting materials: napkins, plates, cups, tableware, place mats

Before You Begin Involve your child in inviting people to lunch or planning a meal for the family. This basic activity may become a routine in your home for every day of the week.

What to Do

1 Before the meal, ask your child what is needed to set the table. Discuss the different objects with which you set your table.

2 Let your child come up with his own game plan, or guide him through the process of setting the table, step-by-step. Your child will need to determine how many people will sit at the table, and then get out a corresponding number of spoons, forks, etc.

3 Once materials have been gathered, set one place. Your child can visually copy the pattern. You might want to talk about what you're doing, using directional words and working step-by-step, for example: "First I lay the place mat on the table. Then I fold a napkin in half, and place it on the left side—see, that's this side—of the place mat. I think it looks best with the point pointing to the left. Beside the napkin goes the fork. Then, to the right . . ."

4 When your child has finished setting the table, thank him for his help. Praise him!

Follow-up Activity Invite your child to set the table regularly. Work together with your child to create a diagram of a place setting to help him remember what he needs and what goes where.

Purposeful counting and one-to-one correspondence are the two vital concepts that setting the table involves. It's also a loving task. The most important "things" in the world to your child are people, and the most important people are generally those found around your table. Table setting is a generous act, requiring consideration of each person. Does the baby get a fork? Who might need an extra napkin? Who gets the wine glasses? Who sits in each chair? Which teacup would Grandma like? There's so much more than math going on here, but math helps your child get the job done.

Watch your child as he masters table setting over time. How does he count things out at first? Is he counting "1, 2, 3" or saying as he pulls each fork from the drawer, "Mom, Dad, me . . ." How does he change his strategy of assembling and arranging items? You can see the gears turning as your child moves into a deeper understanding of the relationship between objects and numerals.

Moving Ahead

Involve your child in the details of meal planning. How many servings do you need for each person? Make this sort of statement to open the problem: "Each person gets one pickle. How many do we need?" Move on to "Each child at this party gets a party hat, a dish of ice cream, and two cookies. How many . . . ?"

Helpful Hint

Buy a plain plastic place mat and a permanent marker, and let your child diagram his own place setting, tracing the items, or drawing them freehand, and labeling them in invented writing.

49 Doll House Furniture

Helps develop: *understanding of structure, proportion, patterns, and construction, flexibility in thinking*

We used big Duplo blocks to make the beds, and paper towels for the sheets. We cut pictures out of magazines to hang on the walls, and used a pot holder for the rug on the floor. The dolls? Clothespins with faces drawn in felt-tip pen and tiny rabbit-fur mice like the ones you buy in pet shops for the cat to play with. I guess it was really a mouse house.

You'll Need

an assortment of odds and ends that can be glued; glue; scissors; other tools and materials depending on the item you're making

Before You Begin

Some children start with the dolls. Some start with the idea of a house. Either way, you need furniture, a roof overhead, and inhabitants. The key question is: "What does this house—or this family—need?"

What to Do

1 Respond to your child's request for dolls, house, or furniture by saying, "I wonder how we could make that?"

2 Wonder with your child about the item in question—say, a kitchen table. How big should it be? How far off the floor should it stand? Who's going to sit at it? What are you going to use for chairs?

3 Guide your child to develop a plan based on the answers to these questions. If she has a doll in mind, get it, and suggest using the doll to determine how tall the table should be. Compare your own table: how high is it on your child? Should it be that high on the doll?

4 Ask your child what materials the table might be made of. Help her to assemble them and to create a plan for how the table will be put together. What will the legs be made of? (Sections of wooden chopsticks? Blocks? Pencil stubs?) What will the top be made of? (Cardboard? A plastic lid from a margarine container? A square of wood?) And what about a tablecloth?

5 Have your child build the table, with assistance from you only as requested. Talk about the process. Let her figure out ways of fastening by gluing or nailing.

6 Finish the process by using the items in a bit of dramatic play.

Follow-up Activities
- Encourage your child to add to her house at will. Put on an addition or do some renovation. Invite your child to move a wall to accommodate more dolls, learning in the process how a space can be rearranged.

- See Activity 21: Box Buildings for help with building houses.

What's Happening

Who says you need a ready-made house or furniture? Just think of the math concepts your child gleans from the process of designing and making her own house, furniture, and even dolls: first, there's the valuable understanding of that process, then there is the form, size, measurement, and function that goes into building. Next time your child wants to make something, she'll feel a little more sure of her ability to do so. And if the effort fails? There's always masking tape to hold the item together. Or encourage her to try again with another material, comparing the effort to the first attempt.

Moving Ahead
Activity 19: Making Models involves creating replicas of actual items to scale. It's a step up from imagining something and eyeballing the dimensions, as was done in this activity.

Helpful Hint
Buy a set of miniature food boxes and cans at a toy store or dime store, and go about filling them with actual food or other materials from your cupboards. You'll only need a little, and it's an interesting and creative exercise for your child to find the miniature substitutes for particular foods, seeing them from a doll's perspective. Cheerios become bagels, white beans become potatoes, beads become peas.

50 Poker Faces

Helps develop: understanding of probability, one-to-one correspondence, concepts of more and less, and basic arithmetic functions

Some people think that mathematicians provide answers, but really, they're more likely to raise questions. The more deeply you go in math, the less certain things become.

You'll Need   playing cards; poker chips; bowl (the "kitty")

Before You Begin   One point of this game is to assess whether your card is higher or lower than your opponent's. So your child needs to understand *less* and *more* in relation to numbers. Familiarize your child with the deck of cards so that he recognizes, for example, that 2 is lower than 8. You may wish to explain the relative values of the face cards, or remove them from the deck to keep things simple.

What to Do

1 Have your child deal ten chips to you, ten to himself.

2 Shuffle the cards, and give them to your child to deal. Ask him to deal them face down, one per player.

3 Ante up: each of you must place a chip in the kitty between you.

4 Show your child how to pick up his card without looking at it and hold it against his forehead, face out, so that you can see it but he can't. You do the same with your card.

5 Look at each other's cards, but not at your own. Do not tell each other what the cards are. Each of you must guess, based on a look at the other's card, whether your card is higher or lower.

6 Take the cards off your foreheads and look at them. If one person is right, he wins all the chips. If more than one person is right, the chips are divided. If no one is right, the chips stay in the kitty until the next round.

- Don't reshuffle the cards for the next game. Just place the used cards face up on the bottom of the deck and move on. Savvy players may begin to base their guesses on the number of cards that have already been played, knowing what might be left.
- To play this game with three, simply add a guess: highest, middle, and lowest.

What's Happening

Your child learns from this game that he has chosen a card from a scale of 2 to 9 or more. When he guesses "higher" or "lower," he makes an assessment based on your card. If it's a 2, he'll learn to surmise that his own card is likely to be higher. Some children will grasp this immediately; they already know a lot about numbers and counting. Others will use this game as experience that will lead them to the knowledge they need.

So much of math is about estimation, about guessing, about assessing the probable outcome of any situation. When you introduce your child to a game with an unknown variable, you give him confidence in his ability to make an educated guess.

Moving Ahead

For older kids, add betting to this game. Both of you think your card is higher? Bet on it. Say your child sees that you have a 4, so your child guesses his card is higher. But you see that your child has an 8, so you're less certain, but are hoping for the best when you guess higher. Let him raise you. He'll soon learn when to bet and when to fold 'em. If he learns at an early age that rash betting can cause him to sell himself short, he probably won't grow up to be a gambler; but he will have a fine grasp of statistical differences and some basic principles of probability.

Helpful Hint

Another good card game involves placing the deck of cards face down and asking your child to guess whether the card turned up will be black or red. Make a pile for correct guesses and incorrect guesses. It's a strange outcome of probability that most people end up with piles of equal size.

51 Mancala

This ancient African game comes in beautiful wooden editions available in toy stores, but it works every bit as well in this homemade version.

You'll Need
the bottom half of an egg carton; a bag of dry beans; two small bowls *or* baskets

Before You Begin
Set up the game: Place the egg carton between you and your child. Place a bowl or basket at each end of the egg carton. These are the *mancalas*. The mancala to your right is yours; the mancala to your child's right (your left) is hers. Place four beans in each cup of the egg carton. Leave the mancalas empty. The egg cups on your side of the carton are yours; those on your child's side are hers.

What to Do
Rules of the game

1 Players take turns. On your turn, take all the beans from any one of your cups and "sow" them as follows: place one in the cup to the right of the one you drew from, the next in the next cup to the right, and so on, moving around the board counterclockwise until the beans are gone. Sow beans one by one in your own cups, your mancala, and your opponent's cups.

- Don't sow a bean in your opponent's mancala.
- If your last bean is sown in your mancala, you get an extra turn.
- If your last bean is sown in an empty cup, you get the beans in your opponent's cup opposite.
- You win the beans that are sown in your mancala. Sow beans only from cups, not from the mancala.
- You're not allowed to take the beans out of a cup to count them.

2 Continue playing until one player runs out of beans in her cups.

- When you run out of beans, your opponent wins all the beans in her cups. They go in her mancala.
- The player with the most beans in her mancala at the end wins.

Follow-up Activity

Play this game again and again. Involve your child in all parts of the game: setting up, playing, and putting away. You'll be surprised how quick both of you get. This really is a game for all ages.

What's Happening

This game has a beautiful simplicity that allows children to really manipulate numbers of objects toward a specific goal. One-to-one correspondence is strongly reinforced as children sow one bean per cup. Mental arithmetic gets a boost from having concrete objects to work with, handle, and study. And then there's strategy. This is not a game in which you will generally have to ponder whether to let your child win.

By involving your child in the setup and cleanup of this game, you help build a scaffolding for basic multiplication concepts. One way of deciding who wins is to take the beans from both mancalas and begin setting up again, each of you working from his or her own end. Your child will soon see the pattern in counting by fours.

Moving Ahead

Up the cup count to five or six beans per cup. This changes the game quite a bit, adds to necessary strategy, makes it all take longer, and introduces a new multiplication concept.

Helpful Hint

Play Mancala with a variety of objects of like size and shape: acorns, seashells, raisins, pennies. This will help your child understand that numbers are constant even when the object being counted changes.

52 Weather Table

Helps develop: methods of recording, naming attributes, representing sets

A week of weather yields math data galore. Help your child keep track of the world around him.

You'll Need   poster board; marker

Before You Begin   Have a discussion of the weather with your child. What does he predict the weather will be for the coming week?

What to Do

1 Discuss the kind of weather that your area experiences. Come up with symbols for three or four weather categories, such as sun, clouds, rain, or snow. I like to use the weather symbols used by the U.S. Weather Service. They can be found in the weather map in most newspapers.

2 Create a table by writing labels or using pictures to mark the weather categories across the top and leaving space to write the days down the side.

3 In the first space, your child can write the day's name and place an X in the category that corresponds to the kind of weather you're having. Try to do this at the same time each day, so you'll have, for example, 11 A.M. weather or 6 P.M. weather.

4 Continue each day, writing the name of the day and marking its weather with an X. Do not fill categories that don't apply; just leave them blank.

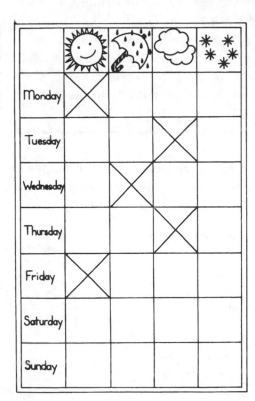

Follow-up Activity   Review your data. Which kind of weather was most prevalent?

What's Happening   So much information comes to us through tables, which are often the clearest way of showing a group of data. As your child fills the table with information he observes around him, he will grow to understand how the rows and columns of a table can illustrate all kinds of facts. Use tables to represent data from other activities, such as Activity 38: Loops and Hoops or Activity 15: Take a Vote, and you'll help your child see how one group of data can be represented in different ways.

Moving Ahead   Take a nature walk and bring home a handful of leaves and flowers. If you can, name them; otherwise, number them. Use them to create a table based on attributes your child determines, such as shape, color, size, smell, or texture. Note that some leaves or flowers will have Xs in more than one category.

Helpful Hint   Use a table to determine whether your dinner each night represents the 4 food groups. Write the names of the food groups—meat and fish, bread and cereals, dairy, fruit and vegetables—across the top, then write the name of the day in the left column. Ask your child to fill in the chart for each meal.

53 Go Fish!

*Every card game has its own protocol,
something valuable in itself for your child to learn.
Go Fish! has a very particular protocol indeed.*

Helps develop:
*matching, under-
standing of sets, strategy,
numeral recognition*

You'll Need   a deck of playing cards

Before You Begin   Decide with your child whether to play for pairs (two of the same denomination) or tricks (four of the same denomination). The key to this is the amount of cards your child can hold in her hand. If the number is low, play for pairs. Each time one of you gets a pair, lay it down on the table. The pile can't be added to with one card, though; players must wait until they have another pair to lay it down.

What to Do   1 Deal seven cards to each player. Turn the remaining cards face down in the center of the table.

2 At the start of her turn, a player asks her opponent for a card, by saying, "Do you have any ———?" (kings, twos, or whatever). She can only ask for a card to match one already held in her hand.

3 If the opponent has what's being asked for, she hands over one card (even if she has others). Then the first player must say, "Fish, fish, I got my wish," and takes another turn.

4 If the opponent does not have the card, she says, "Go fish." The first player draws a card from the deck. Again, if she gets what she asked for, she says, "Fish, fish, I got my wish." If she gets a card that is not the denomination she asked for, but that does match a card in her hand, she says, "Fish, fish, I did not get my wish, but I did get a match." She doesn't get another turn. She does, however, place her match face up in front of her on the table.

5 If the card she chooses matches nothing in her hand, she must simply hold onto it.

6 The game ends when one player runs out of cards in her hand or the deck runs out of cards, whichever comes first.

Follow-up Activity   This game can be played with three or four people. Each player asks for cards from the player to her left. If she gets her wish, she asks the next person to the left.

What's Happening   A child who plays Go Fish is learning about matching pairs and about holding and arranging a hand of cards. She is also learning when and how to ask for cards she wants and determining (through observation) that each trick of cards has four suits.

Moving Ahead   Make your own deck of cards by cutting index cards in half. Each trick will be four cards with addition or subtraction problems whose totals are the same number, for example: 4 + 2, 7 − 1, 8 − 2, 3 + 3. Players must ask for cards by giving the total: "Do you have any sixes?"

Helpful Hint   Children who have trouble holding a hand of cards can stack them, pinch them with a clothespin, fan them out, then hold up the clothes-pin.

54 Oh, You Beautiful Doll!

Helps develop: *problem solving, understanding of spatial relationships and perimeters*

The earliest paper dolls were handmade by parents for their children. Handmade dolls can have custom features and clothing, and you can't beat the price.

You'll Need light cardboard *or* recycled manila folders; drawing paper; scissors; markers *or* crayons; pencil

Before You Begin Talk to your child about what paper dolls are, how they are made, and how they are played with.

What to Do

1 Ask your child what sort of paper doll he would like to make. Have him draw a picture or describe the doll.

2 Discuss what a paper doll needs to have in order to function: flat feet or a pedestal, shoulders free of hair, and waist or arms positioned so that they can hold up clothing tabs.

3 Help your child draw the outline of his doll on a sheet of cardboard. You might draw a doll shape for him to fill in, provide another paper doll to trace, or have him draw freehand.

4 Have your child cut out the paper doll, fill in its features, and draw underwear. Make a stand or add a strip of cardboard that fits into slots in the doll's base.

5 Have the child use the doll as a template to trace for clothes. One way to do this is to trace the doll's form on paper in pencil, then have the child draw a dress or suit on the shape.

6 Talk about the need for tabs to hold the clothes on the doll. Which parts of the doll will hold the tabs? How many tabs are needed? Have your child add tabs to the clothes.

7 Have your child cut out the doll's clothes and try them on the doll.

Follow-up Activity Encourage your child to try copying a favorite outfit of his own for the doll to wear.

What's Happening *Creating a paper doll that stands up and clothes that stay on requires understanding of weight, structure, and support. When your child learns these concepts through experimentation—trial and error—he also gains vital understanding of the process of building something that works. "I made it myself" is a statement of pride and confidence. Let your child gain confidence and skill in making something basic, and he'll move more easily toward figuring out more complex tasks.*

Moving Ahead Try using different materials for clothes. Clear acetate, felt, foil, magazine pages, and so on, all have their own special properties that will add to the problem of creating clothes and make the process continually interesting.

Helpful Hint To store dolls, use an envelope with a window or create a windowed envelope by cutting a square from a used envelope and covering it with waxed paper or plastic wrap. This allows your child to see what's inside.

55 Give Me a Hand

*Words, and word problems, are about
communication. Let communication come first,
and the math will follow.*

You'll Need four people; paper and pencil

Before You Begin Try this with three or four children, or adults with an interest in math and a sense of humor. (That's everybody, isn't it?) Ask them all to greet one another in any way they wish.

What to Do

1 Ask your child, "If everybody here shook hands with everybody else, how many handshakes would there be?"

2 Listen to her guess. Make no comment.

3 Now organize the handshakes. Have each person shake hands with everybody else. Help your child keep track (make a mark on the paper with the pencil, or on the ground with a stick) of the handshakes.

4 Talk about her guess and the outcome. Discuss what she assumed would happen beforehand and how her ideas changed when she saw how the handshakes worked out in reality.

Follow-up Activity Add another person to your group. Based on what you know about four people shaking hands, how many handshakes will there be when there are five people?

What's Happening This is the kind of problem that you see a lot in higher-level math such as algebra. But why wait? Research has shown that little kids can understand algebraic concepts (as well as concepts from geometry, trigonometry, and so on). Like anything else, algebra is easier to understand in concrete form—and the mental hops and leaps this handshaking problem requires are fun and stimulating to work out in real life.

Moving Ahead   Ask your child to diagram or draw the handshakes to figure out how many there would be if there were three people, six people, and so on. A diagram for four people might look like the one below.

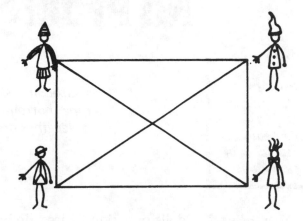

Helpful Hint   Boost this concept with a card game such as I Doubt You or Old Maid, which require passing a set number of cards between players. Any card game that involves dealing is helpful. See Activity 53: Go Fish!.

56 Word Problems? No Problem!

*H*elps develop: use of language to represent math relationships, computation, understanding of arithmetic functions

Barbie has six pairs of leggings. Skipper borrows two. How many pairs of leggings does Barbie have left?

You'll Need dolls or action figures, doll clothes, cars, fake food, and other accessories

Before You Begin Do this activity as a natural outgrowth of time spent playing with your child and his favorite toy figures—Power Rangers, Barbies, Playmobil guys, or whatever else he prefers.

What to Do 1 As you're playing with your child, think of a math problem that can be expressed in words. Make it something that's part of your play. Here are some examples:

- "I wonder how many Barbies can fit in that car? Four are already in. Can Ken and Stacey get in too?"
- "So many shoes! Are there enough for all the dolls?"
- "Are there more bad guys, or more Power Rangers?"
- "If every Power Ranger can overpower two bad guys, how many can they all defeat at once?"

2 Once you have your child interested in the question, act it out with the dolls. "Stacey can fit in, and that makes five. But there are only five seats. Ken, you'll have to walk, buddy."

3 Talk about the answer to the problem and how it was figured out.

Follow-up Activity Think of everyday word problems to enact actively with your child. These can spring from arithmetic problems in your child's schoolbook or from your own mind. "3 + 4? Let's work it out. Go get three raisins out of the box. Now get four more. Count 'em up. How many?"

What's Happening Understanding of any math function should come from experience that is concrete first, graphic second, symbolic third. When you add spoken language, you help your child make the transition from concrete or graphic representations of a problem to symbolic representations of a problem. Once they make this transition, many children find great pleasure in realizing that they can read math problems, interpret them, and solve them. Still, being able to represent a problem symbolically is no indication of the ability to solve it abstractly. Through this activity, you give your child a tool, a strategy for figuring out any problem concretely.

Moving Ahead Take the problem you worked out with the dolls and encourage your child to draw it out on paper. "Remember what the car looked like before Ken and Stacey tried to get in? Can you draw it? Where are Ken and Stacey?" Your child may write *4* beneath the car and *2* beneath Ken and Stacey, then add the answer, *6*, and the symbols that show what took place.

Helpful Hint Within reason, *do* let your child play with his food. For example, have him guess how many slices his apple might divide into, and confirm his prediction by cutting the apple and counting the slices. Once the number is established, allow him to group and regroup the apple slices before eating them. Ask, from time to time, "How many are left?"

57 Concentration

The younger of two sisters was so good at this game that the older sister finally asked her how she did it. "You're trying to memorize the cards," the younger sister said. "I'm seeing them floating in their places."

Helps develop: *numeral recognition, matching, strategy, analysis of patterns*

You'll Need a deck of playing cards

Before You Begin Play this with a child who can match up like letters and numerals, even if she can't necessarily name them. You may want to play with just half a deck of cards, so that each card has only one denominational match, then move on to the full deck (or a double deck, for a real challenge) later.

What to Do

1 Lay all the cards out face down in a grid pattern of your choosing.

2 Take turns turning over any two cards. If the two cards match (are the same number or rank), you get another turn. If they don't match, replace them face down in the exact spot they came from.

3 Matched cards get removed from the game and laid down before the player who won them, face up. The remaining cards are not moved at all.

4 The game is over when there are no cards left.

Follow-up Activity Play this game in teams, two players per team. The first player picks up the first card, the second player picks up the second card.

What's Happening *Success at this game depends a little bit on luck, a lot on memory. It's what you do with your memory that counts. It's interesting to see the different methods each person has of playing this game. Some do rely purely on chance—and can do surprisingly well, considering the odds. Others, like that younger sister, have a real strategy, a mental grid with cards that fit neatly into it. Still others recall the relationship between cards: a king next to a 2, a 3 next to the corner card, and so on.*

Moving Ahead An interesting way to vary this game is to spread the cards out, in the same grid pattern, over the floor instead of on a tabletop. Putting a lot of distance between the cards makes for a different kind of visualization. Ask your child to play this way, then compare the floor game with the tabletop version. Which is harder? Is the strategy for playing very different? Does touching the cards help you remember where they are?

Helpful Hint Play Concentration with other types of cards—lotto cards cut from magazines like *Ladybug* or picture cards from Animal Match. Younger children, especially, may find pictures easier to recall and match than symbols.

58 Time: On Your Side

Helps develop: concept of time and time measurement

"After lunch" may mean far more to a child than "at two o'clock." Children do indeed live on a separate plane.

You'll Need a jar with a narrow neck; ice cream cone with pointed tip *or* paper coffee filter; paper cup; sand; water

Before You Begin Ask your child how long he thinks it takes him to do something he does every day: put on shoes, climb the stairs, walk backward down the hall, and so on.

What to Do

1 Suggest timing your child as he does a specific activity. Ask him, "I wonder how we can figure out how long it takes?"

2 Your child may suggest simply counting out loud, or keeping his eyes on the clock's second hand as he does the activity. Do those things, then suggest another way.

3 Say, "Here's an idea." Use a pin or sharp knife to poke a hole in the bottom of the ice cream cone or coffee filter. Stand it in the neck of the jar so that the tip reaches halfway down. Fill the cone with sand.

4 See how much sand comes down before your child completes his task.

5 Ask your child if he can think of another way to measure time.

Follow-up Activity Measurement methods can also include placing a paper cup in the mouth of your jar. Make a pinhole, and fill the paper cup with water. Count the drips. You could sing or recite a poem and see if you finish before all the water drips out. Also try doing a task in tandem with your child. "Can you pick up all the toys in the time it takes me to put away the dishes?"

What's Happening

As with other standard measurements, seconds, minutes, and hours are meaningless before the concept that time can be measured is gotten across. In most cases, children who can supposedly tell time don't have an understanding of time; they just can read numbers on a dial. Children will learn first how the clock looks when it's time for something special to happen: bedtime, for example. Children may also begin to grasp the concept of time by reference to something they have experienced, for example, television shows. You may tell your child, "Traveling from New York to Washington, D.C., takes as long as three Sesame Streets and a Mister Rogers." Talk to your child about time, and get him to measure it with you through words, chants, activities, and clocks.

Moving Ahead

Bring your child to a better understanding of our standard time measurements by timing various activities by the clock and graphing them to make comparisons.

Helpful Hint

Teach your child to take his pulse. It's a rhythm similar to the ticks of a clock that he can use to time activities, and it's also a key to discussions of body clocks and rhythms. Of course it's also a good health skill to have at his fingertips!

59 ...And Math Is Woven In

Helps develop: sense of the structure of patterns, rhythmic moving, understanding a process

*String for the warp,
All nature for the weft,
When hands are all finished
A tapestry's left.*

You'll Need   two straight sticks that are thick as a thumb and 3 feet (1 m) long; heavy brown twine; natural materials for weaving

Before You Begin   Gather natural weaving materials from an outdoor area. Include leaves, branches, grasses, cattails, anything that is of a length of at least 12 inches (30 cm) and is flexible enough to become part of a fabric. You can also use yarn, ribbons, fabrics—whatever you please.

What to Do

1 Measure and cut 20 pieces of twine approximately 4 feet (120 cm) long.

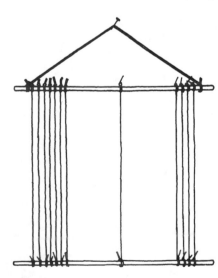

2 Tie one end of each string to one stick, and the other end to the second stick. Tie ten strings on in this manner; then attach a string to the top stick to act as a hanger. Hang your loom up and continue tying on strings. When you've finished, your loom is ready for weaving. The strings are called the warp.

3 Show your child how to weave her arm through the strings of the loom, over one string and under the next. Then have her weave each finger of a hand through, alternating so that one finger goes under a string and the next goes over it.

4 Begin to weave your grasses and other materials through the warp. Now you have the weft. The combination of warp and weft makes a fabric or tapestry.

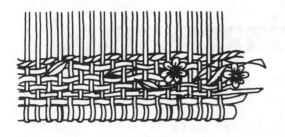

What's nice about a wall loom is that you don't have to weave in any sequence. The basic pattern, should you choose to follow it, is to go over and under with each strand of material, and when you make the next line of weaving to switch to under and over. Adjust the space between strands to your taste. Fluff out tassels of grass or heads of dried flowers to make your fabric three-dimensional.

What's Happening

Through weaving your child gains insight into the processes that work to create clothing and other fabric items. By replicating a pattern, she takes in vital information about rhythm, structure, and the purpose of fabric. As she experiments with patterns, "just to see what will happen if . . . ," she gets ownership of a creative process. She'll also pick up basic concepts of odd/even alternating, counting, and measurement.

As a group activity, this project has few parallels. You can make it a seasonal thing to be repeated at different times of the year as a showcase for different people's tastes in materials, and a way to involve children in a collaborative effort.

Moving Ahead

Provide your child with a manufactured child's loom—the type that comes with big bags of loops. Yes, there are children's versions of real, more authentic looms, but a child should first get her hands on the basic patterns and procedures of weaving through laying the warp and incorporating the weft in this most basic of toys.

Helpful Hint

To preserve your natural weaving materials—grass, branches, cattails, and so on,—let them drink up a bucket of glycerine water. First, cut the stems and smash them with a hammer. Make a solution of glycerine (available from drugstores) and water, and leave the natural materials standing in the bucket for three days. (This process may discolor red or orange leaves.) The materials will work better if they are pressed in a book before being incorporated into the tapestry.

60 Diagrammed Doings

*This is the paper that holds the drawing
that shows the diagram
that gives directions
to build the house
that your child built!*

You'll Need   interlocking blocks such as Lego, Duplo, K'nex, or Mottik; paper and pencil

Before You Begin   With your child, use a diagram that comes with commercial blocks like Legos or Duplos to create a structure. Talk about each part of the diagram, what it shows, and how it directs you to put blocks together. Save this activity until your child has built his own construction freehand.

What to Do

1 Admire your child's work. Suggest that he make a diagram of his structure, and point out that there are two reasons he might want to do this: to save the structure and to replicate it. Remind him of the diagrams used to show people how to make block structures.

2 Your child's age will determine the level of complexity of his diagram. He may make a drawing of the finished product. He may draw the construction in a few stages. Or, he may start with a sheet that shows all the materials needed, and move up from ground level to the finished product, step-by-step.

3 Ask your child, "If I were making this model, what would I need to do first?" Let your child come up with a numbering system or additional drawings to show the stages.

4 Use your child's drawing to re-create the model.

Follow-up Activities
- Turn the tables. Create a simple diagram of your own for your child to follow.
- Keep a book of diagrams of your child's constructions.
- Suggest that your child make a diagram for another child as a gift.

What's Happening
A diagram that shows how to make something must take into account the movement required. By diagramming something he has done through moving, your child learns to show the main steps, number the movements, and label the parts. All of these methods encourage children to see what Einstein worked all those years to do: Taking an action, freezing it, recording it, and even replicating it. What's more, children who learn to diagram three-dimensional constructions are learning a language of representing space in two dimensions—a good foundation for geometry, engineering, and architecture.

Moving Ahead
Experiment with the drawing program on your computer to create a palette of block shapes that your child can use to re-create his block constructions on the screen. While this is easiest to do with basic block shapes (rectangles, squares, and triangles) in various colors, whizzes may be able to draw less regular shapes (propellers, wheels, and so on) that can be cut and pasted into the picture.

Helpful Hint
If you've lost the diagrams that come with your Lego blocks, or if you received your Legos as hand-me-downs or yard sale purchases and have no diagrams, you can get them by calling a local Lego representative. You can get the phone number from a toy store.

Activities Index

About the Authors

Marlene Barron is an internationally known educator and authority on the educational and developmental needs of preschool and elementary school children. She holds a Ph.D. in Early Childhood and Elementary Education. Her focus is early literacy development. She is Head of West Side Montessori School in New York City and a professor at New York University. Dr. Barron gives frequent lectures and workshops on early childhood education around the country and also publishes articles in professional journals. She is the author of *I Learn to Read and Write the Way I Learn to Talk: A Very First Book About Whole Language.*

Karen Romano Young is a writer specializing in educational materials for children, teachers, and parents. Formerly an editor at Scholastic, she has written for the National Geographic Society and Children's Television Workshop. Her work has appeared in books, magazines, and other media. Ms. Young holds a B.S. in elementary education and is the mother of three children.